Series Editor:
Paul Wehman, Ph.D.

Adulthood Series

TRANSITION
PLANNING FOR
Culturally and
Linguistically
Diverse Youth

The Brookes
Transition to
Adulthood Series

TRANSITION PLANNING FOR
Culturally and Linguistically Diverse Youth

by

Gary Greene, Ph.D.
California State University, Long Beach

·P·A·U·L·H·
BROOKES
PUBLISHING CO.®

Baltimore • London • Sydney

Paul H. Brookes Publishing Co.
Post Office Box 10624
Baltimore, Maryland 21285-0624
USA

www.brookespublishing.com

Typeset by Auburn Associates, Inc., Baltimore, Maryland.
Manufactured in the United States of America by
Victor Graphics, Inc., Baltimore, Maryland.

The individuals described in this book are composites or real people whose situations are masked and are based on the authors' experiences. In all instances, names and identifying details have been changed to protect confidentiality.

Library of Congress Cataloging-in-Publication Data
Greene, Gary.
    Transition planning for culturally and linguistically diverse youth / by Gary Greene.
        p.   cm. – (The Brookes transition to adulthood series)
    Includes bibliographical references and index.
    ISBN-13: 978-1-59857-159-2 (pbk.)
    ISBN-10: 1-59857-159-1 (pbk.)
1. Minority people with disabilities–Education (Secondary)–United States.   2. Minority people with disabilities–Counseling of–United States.   3. Minority people with disabilities–Vocational guidance–United States.   4. School-to-work transition–United States.   I. Title.
LC4031.G684 2011
370.1130973–dc22   2011015132

British Library Cataloguing in Publication data are available from the British Library.

2015   2014   2013   2012   2011

10   9   8   7   6   5   4   3   2   1

Contents

Series Preface vii
Editorial Advisory Board ix
About the Author xi
Preface xiii
Acknowledgments xv

1   Challenges Faced by Culturally and Linguistically
    Diverse Families and Youth with Disabilities During the
    Transition Years 1

    What Is Meant by the Terms *Cultural Diversity* and
       Cultural and Linguistic Diversity?
    What Are the Effects of Low Socioeconomic Status and
       Poverty on the Transition Experiences of CLD Youth
       with Disabilities?
    What Are the Experiences of CLD Families of Youth with
       Disabilities in the Transition Planning Process?

2   Culturally Responsive Transition Planning and
    Recommended Practices 23

    What Are the Key Elements and Skills Involved in Culturally
       Responsive Collaboration in Special Education?
    What Are Recommended Practices in Culturally Responsive
       Transition Planning with CLD Families of Youth with
       Disabilities, and What Do These Look Like in Public
       Schools?

3   Transition Individualized Education Programs and Summary
    of Functional Performance Documents for Culturally
    and Linguistically Diverse Family Examples 55

    What Is the Rationale for Writing Transition IEPs and SOPs
       for Youth with Disabilities?
    What Are the Legal Requirements of IDEA 2004 with
       Respect to Transition IEPs and SOPs?

How Can Special Education and Transition Personnel
    Conduct Transition Assessments to Obtain Information
    Needed for Writing Culturally Responsive Transition IEPs
    and SOPs?
What Types of Transition Programs and Services Are
    Available in High School and Beyond that Meet the
    Needs of CLD Families and Youth with Disabilities?
What Are Examples of Quality, Culturally Responsive
    Transition IEPs and SOPs?

4   The Role of Teacher Leadership in Promoting
    Organizational Change and Successful Transition for
    Culturally and Linguistically Diverse Youth with Disabilities 93

    What Is the Definition and What Are the Characteristics of
        Teacher Leadership?
    How Can Teacher Leadership Be Promoted in the Public
        Schools?
    What Strategies Can Be Used by Teacher Leaders to
        Promote Organizational Change in Their Schools
        or Districts?

5   Epilogue: What Do We Know, What Have We Learned, and
    Where Do We Go from Here to Help Culturally and
    Linguistically Diverse Families and Youth with
    Disabilities in the Transition Process? 117

    What Do We Know About the Transition Experiences of
        CLD Families and Youth with Disabilities?
    What Have We Learned About How to Support CLD
        Families of Youth with Disabilities During the Transition
        Years?
    Where Do We Go from Here?

References 125

For Further Information 131

Index 138

Series Preface

The Brookes Transition to Adulthood Series was developed for the purpose of meeting the critical educational needs of students with disabilities who will be moving from school to adulthood. It is no longer acceptable to simply equip a student with a set of isolated life skills that may or may not be relevant to his or her adult life. Nor is it sufficient to treat the student as if he or she will remain unchanged throughout life. As we allow for growth and change in real-life environments, so must we allow for growth and change in the individuals who will operate within the environments. Today, transition must concern itself with the whole life pattern of each student as it relates to his or her future. However, integrating the two constructs of self and the real adult world for one student at a time is not always straightforward. It requires skills and knowledge. It requires a well-thought-out, well-orchestrated team effort. It takes individualization, ingenuity, perseverance, and more.

The results of these first-rate efforts can be seen when they culminate in a student with a disability who exits school prepared to move to his or her life beyond the classroom. Unfortunately, though, this does not always happen. This is because transition has become a splintered concept, too weighted down by process and removed from building on the student's aspirations and desires for "a good life." However, it does not have to be this way.

This book series is designed to help the teachers, transition specialists, rehabilitation counselors, community service providers, administrators, policy makers, other professionals, and families who are looking for useful information on a daily basis by translating the evidence-based transition research into practice. Each volume addresses specific objectives that are related to the all-important and overarching goal of helping students meet the demands of school and society and gain a greater understanding of themselves so that they are equipped for success in the adult world.

Editorial Advisory Board

About the Author

Gary Greene, Ph.D., Professor of Special Education, California State University, Long Beach, 1250 Bellflower Boulevard, Long Beach, California 90840

Dr. Greene is a tenured full professor of special education at California State University, Long Beach, where he trains public school special education teachers in how to accommodate youth with special needs in general and special education classrooms. He also works as a special education consultant for the U.S. Department of State, Division of Overseas Schools. Dr. Greene has traveled extensively throughout the world conducting international school site reviews, as well as special education teacher and parent trainings. He has been teaching and supervising classroom teachers since the mid-1980s. Dr. Greene has a strong background in teaching youth with disabilities, having worked as a resource specialist for 10 years in the public schools with children with learning disabilities. He has teaching credentials in both general and special education, a bachelor's degree in psychology from the University of California, Los Angeles, a master's degree in special education from the University of Southern California, and a doctoral degree in special education from the University of California, Riverside. He also holds an administrative services credential. Dr. Greene has an extensive list of publications and has conducted numerous local, state, national, and international presentations on a variety of subjects related to special education. In 2003, he coauthored a college textbook on the topic of transition of youth with disabilities from school to quality adult life titled *Pathways to Successful Transition for Youth with Disabilities* (with Carol A. Kochhar-Bryant, Merrill-Prentice Hall). A second edition of that book was published in 2009 titled *Pathways to Successful Transition for Youth with Disabilities: A Developmental Approach* (Merrill/Pearson).

Preface

Writing a book on the subject of transition for culturally and linguistically diverse (CLD) youth with disabilities and their families is an exciting yet daunting task. The topic of cultural and linguistic diversity is very complex and must be approached in an intellectually careful and sensitive manner. With that said, I want readers to know that I have been involved with the topic of transition of youth with disabilities for more than 25 years. Beginning in 1987, I trained more than 100 transition specialists at California State University, Long Beach. I was hired to coordinate a federally funded personnel preparation grant that provided coursework and practicum experience in transition services to secondary level special education teachers and various adult transition service agency personnel (i.e., from vocational education, vocational rehabilitation, supported employment, and regional center developmental disability programs). The subject of transition was relatively new to me then, given my 10-year special education teacher experience as a resource specialist working with students with learning disabilities in the public schools. Shortly thereafter, transition became a federal priority with the authorization of the Individuals with Disabilities Education Act (IDEA) of 1990 (PL 101-476); it was an exciting time to be involved in transition training.

My passion, knowledge, and expertise in transition have grown tremendously over the course of my career. I have taught graduate courses on the subject; published articles, training materials, and books on transition; served as Journal Editor for *Career Development for Exceptional Individuals*; and conducted state, regional, and national trainings on the topic. Recently I've served as a paid legal consultant to public school districts involved in settling transition-related disputes with families of transition-age youth with disabilities. It's been quite an exciting career and one that has led to the writing of this book.

With this in mind, let me offer some final information as to how I became interested in the transition of CLD youth with disabilities. As stated previously, I live and work in southern California, an extremely culturally and linguistically diverse region of the United States. It became apparent to me in the late 1980s and early 1990s that, although much was being written on the subject of special education for CLD youth with disabilities (i.e., issues related to special education assessment, placement, and programs and services), relatively few publications focused on the topic of transition of CLD youth with disabilities. In fact,

I published one of the first articles on this subject (Greene & Nefsky, 1999). I later wrote an entire chapter on the topic in the first edition of the textbook *Pathways to Successful Transition for Youth with Disabilities* (Greene & Kochhar-Bryant, 2003). In the spring of 2009, I conducted a presentation on the topic of best practices in transition of CLD youth with disabilities at a national convention for the Council for Exceptional Children. I was approached by Paul H. Brookes Publishing Co. with an offer to write a specialty book on this subject. I was both honored and intrigued by this unique opportunity. I was asked to write a book that would be not only practical and user friendly for teachers, families, and adult service providers of CLD youth with disabilities but also research based and scholarly in its content and presentation. I believe the book that I have produced effectively meets these objectives. It is my sincere hope that as a result of reading this book, professionals will be able to develop strong partnerships and practice culturally responsive collaboration with CLD families of youth with disabilities in the transition process, resulting in quality adult lives for CLD youth with disabilities.

REFERENCES

Greene, G., & Kochhar-Bryant, C.A. (2003). *Pathways to successful transition for youth with disabilities.* Upper Saddle River, NJ: Merrill-Prentice Hall.

Greene, G., & Nefsky, P. (1996). Transition for culturally and linguistically diverse youth with disabilities: Closing the gaps. *Multiple Voices for Ethnically Diverse Exceptional Learners, 3*(1), 15–24.

Individuals with Disabilities Education Act (IDEA) of 1990, PL 101-476, 20 U.S.C. §§ 1400 *et seq.*

Acknowledgments

I would like to acknowledge Don Lo'Presti, a high school English teacher and father of one of my lifelong high school friends. It was Don who inspired me to enter the field of education and care about kids who were from culturally and linguistically diverse backgrounds. The high school I attended in my youth was extremely culturally and linguistically diverse, and Don really cared about these students.

I also want to acknowledge Dr. Leonard Albright and Dr. Charles Kokaska, the two faculty members at California State University, Long Beach (CSULB), who wrote the federally funded Office of Special Education and Rehabilitative Services grant that led to my being hired as Coordinator of the Graduate Transition Services Training Program. These individuals gave me my start in this field. I also wish to thank my late wife, Corinne Beacham-Greene, a vocational special needs specialist who introduced me to these individuals shortly after I completed my doctorate in special education. She helped me fulfill my dream of becoming a college professor.

I further wish to acknowledge my colleagues in the special education program at CSULB. We are such a caring and committed group of professionals and have influenced the lives of countless numbers of special education teachers and students with disabilities, many of whom come from culturally and linguistically diverse backgrounds.

Finally, I wish to acknowledge two family members, the first of whom is my Uncle Mort. Mort is 90 years old and is as sharp as a tack! He constantly engages me in political conversations because we are on opposite ends of the political spectrum. Our dialogue is always intellectual, honest, and respectful. This is how dialogue should be in this country; clearly one of my intents in writing this book is to stimulate dialogue. Equally important, however, has been Mort's interest in my work. Every time he sees me, he asks, "How's the book coming?" Thank you, Uncle Mort, for being who you are!

Last, I wish to acknowledge my wife, Linda. She has given me a new spark and passion in life and the promise of a happy future. Linda has been my cheerleader and source of support and encouragement throughout the writing of this book. She also served as my editor! Thanks for being my loving partner, for giving me the time and space needed in the summer of 2010 to write this book, and for all of the good times to come. I love you dearly!

This book is dedicated to families and youth with disabilities who come from culturally and linguistically diverse backgrounds. Many of us in this country have no idea of the challenges you face on a daily basis as families pursuing quality lives in the United States. It is my hope that this book will shed some light on your circumstances and result in improved collaboration and partnerships between you and the professionals with whom you interact in pursuit of quality adult lives for your children with disabilities.

1

Challenges Faced by Culturally and Linguistically Diverse Families and Youth with Disabilities During the Transition Years

The "main dream"…seemed to reflect the "American dream" [which was to have] "a good family, be successful, have a job I like, a nice house, be happy with what I'm doing. Someone I love there, a couple of kids. Have freedom, freedom to do everything I want to do, like travel a lot."

—D. Leake and R. Boone (2007, p. 111)

The opening quote from a youth with a disability comes from an article by Leake and Boone (2007), who studied multicultural perspectives on self-determination in youth with disabilities, their parents, and their teachers. It appropriately summarizes how many people living in the United States define a quality adult life: 1) access to affordable housing in a safe neighborhood; 2) quality schools that provide a good education; 3) employment opportunities that offer a decent hourly wage or salary, along with benefits and the opportunity for career advancement; 4) access to quality health care; 5) close family, friends, and social and interpersonal networks; 6) easy access to one's community; and 7) enjoyable recreation and leisure activities.

Unfortunately for individuals with disabilities, particularly those who are culturally and linguistically diverse (CLD), achieving a quality adult life can be very challenging. Evidence for this exists in early follow-up transition studies that found that large numbers of students with disabilities who exited public schools did not successfully make the transition to a quality adult life. Many of these individuals were leading segregated, nonproductive lives; were not actively engaged in daily activities; and lacked equal opportunity for employment (Blackorby & Wagner, 1996; Edgar, 1991; Halloran, 1993; Hasazi, Gordon, & Roe, 1985). The National Longitudinal Transition Studies (NLTS-1 and NLTS-2) found that, compared with their peers without disabilities, youth with disabilities continued to lag behind in terms of indicators of a quality adult life (Blackorby & Wagner, 1996; NLTS-2, 2005). This is particularly true for CLD youth with disabilities. The NLTS-1 found that minority status was an additional predictor of poor adult life outcomes in the areas of employment, wages, postsecondary school attendance, and independent living for African American and Hispanic youth with disabilities compared with their White peers with disabilities less than 2 years and 3–5 years after exiting school (see Table 1.1). The NLTS-2 found that White youth with disabilities had higher overall rates of engagement (i.e., in postsecondary education, vocational training) or employment than did African American youth with disabilities and higher rates of employment and postsecondary education than did African American and Hispanic youth with disabilities (see Table 1.2).

Why is this so? What possible explanations exist for the poorer transition outcomes of CLD youth with disabilities compared with their White peers with disabilities? This chapter offers a review of the transition literature on the challenges faced by CLD families of youth with disabilities during the transition years and the transition planning process. The chapter begins with a discussion of the construct of *cultural and linguistic diversity*. This construct is quite complex and involves much more than the color of one's skin or the language spoken at home. Since the mid-1990s, numerous articles have been published in the special education literature on the subject of CLD children with disabilities in the public schools. Some experts consider these articles to be overly simplistic and stereotypical (i.e., the articles focus primarily on findings and discussions of the overrepresentation and underrepresentation of certain racial or ethnic groups in special education; see Harry, 1992; Smith & Tyler, 2010). Following the discussion of cultural and linguistic diversity, I present a brief review of the relationship between socioeconomic status (SES) and the transition to a quality adult life. Finally, a comprehensive review of the literature on the transition experiences of CLD youth with disabilities makes up the bulk of the chapter. Much of the literature reviewed presents the words and experiences of CLD families of youth with disabilities in the transition planning process. I identify and discuss common themes in this

Table 1.1. National Longitudinal Transition Study–1 data on transition outcomes of minority and nonminority youth with disabilities

Transition outcome	< 2 years	3–5 years
	%	
Competitive employment		
Whites	53.1	60.8
African Americans	25.5	47.3
Hispanics	49.4	50.5
Earnings > $6/hour		
Whites	8.7	46.3
African Americans	14.2	13.7
Hispanics	0.1	25.0
Postsecondary school attendance		
Whites	14.8	27.5
African Americans	12.7	23.2
Hispanics	9.9	27.7
Independent living		
Whites	13.4	42.3
African Americans	5.1	25.5
Hispanics	15.2	31.1

Source: Blackorby and Wagner (1996).

Table 1.2.   National Longitudinal Transition Study–2 data on transition outcomes of minority and nonminority youth with disabilities

Transition outcome	Within 4 years of leaving school (%)
Overall rate of engagement	
Whites	89
African Americans	67
Employment only	
Whites	39.9
African Americans	16.4
Hispanics	41.5
Employment and postsecondary education	
Whites	34.4
African Americans	24.7
Hispanics	21.0

Source: Newman, Wagner, Cameto, and Knokey (2009).

literature and highlight implications for school personnel interacting with CLD families of youth with disabilities in the transition years and the planning process.

WHAT IS MEANT BY THE TERMS *CULTURAL DIVERSITY* AND *CULTURAL AND LINGUISTIC DIVERSITY?*

Barrera and Corso (2003) presented an excellent discussion of the terms *cultural diversity* and *cultural and linguistic diversity,* which they considered synonymous. (These terms are also used synonymously throughout this book.) They noted that the term *cultural diversity* is used by many to "identify differences that are perceived to stem from culture," focusing on racial and ethnic heritage or identity differences "without examining or controlling for actual differences in behaviors, languages, values, and beliefs" (p. 5). They further pointed out that cultural diversity is not a static quality, cannot be reliably determined by ethnicity alone, and should not be looked at as a "risk factor that must somehow be lessened or reduced" (p. 5). When education professionals and practitioners make any of these assumptions, this can potentially lead to labeling and stereotyping, which limits their ability to respect the diverse practices of others and to rely on these individuals as a helpful resource. The authors pointed out that cultural diversity and people who are considered culturally diverse are relative because "no single person can be said to be diverse, culturally or otherwise, except in reference to other persons or environments" (p. 6). Cultural diversity, then, is not based on ethnicity or an individual characteristic, nor is it defined by a given cultural group or community. Rather, these are only indicators of cultural diversity. Instead, Barrera and Corso (2005) suggested that cultural diversity is defined and characterized by the interactions and comparisons between people within a given environment rather than a trait or characteristic that resides within a given individual.

The challenges involved with interacting with people from a different culture in a strange or uncomfortable environment can produce emotional stress and discomfort. For example, consider an individualized education program (IEP) team discussing a postsecondary goal of independent living for a Latina student with a disability whose mother wants her to keep living at home and helping to care for the family. Barrera and Kramer (1997, as cited in Barrera & Corso, 2003) described this as a *culture bump,* an experience of cognitive and emotional dissonance between people of differing values, beliefs, and worldviews. It is this context that forms the basis of the discussion in this chapter and throughout this book. A potential explanatory variable for the poor transition outcomes of CLD youth with disabilities is in the cultural bumps that occur when CLD families interact with school professionals who differ in their beliefs, values, and worldviews regarding transition. This disconnect subsequently can result in lower quality transition planning and delivery of transition services to CLD youth with disabilities. Trainor (2007) suggested that person-centered planning with CLD youth requires effort to know the student within his or her community.

WHAT ARE THE EFFECTS OF LOW SOCIOECONOMIC STATUS AND POVERTY ON THE TRANSITION EXPERIENCES OF CLD YOUTH WITH DISABILITIES?

A high percentage of minorities have a low SES, as evidenced by data from the U.S. Census Bureau (2001). The poverty rate is 11% for Asian Americans/Pacific Islanders, 23% for Latinos, 24% for African Americans, and 26% for American Indians, compared with 8% for Whites. A strong negative correlation exists between poverty and the quality of adult life. People living in poverty often have limited or no access to quality health care, prenatal care, or adequate nutrition. Further effects of poverty are low-quality housing; transiency; homelessness; and limited access to high-paying jobs, long-term job security, career advancement, and employee benefits. Children living in poverty frequently have little or no access to high-quality preschool programs, attend substandard schools, and drop out of school at a higher rate. Often young adults living in poverty do not have the means to pay for a college education and are forced to enter the work force in order to meet their basic survival needs. Opportunities for employment are limited for individuals without advanced education and training. All of these effects of poverty clearly can have a lifelong impact on individuals, beginning in the school years with potential learning and behavior problems and continuing into adulthood with lower quality employment and life satisfaction outcomes (Smith & Tyler, 2010). Hence, it can be argued that a direct relationship exists between SES and the transition to a quality adult life independent of one's cultural or linguistic background.

WHAT ARE THE EXPERIENCES OF CLD FAMILIES OF YOUTH WITH DISABILITIES IN THE TRANSITION PLANNING PROCESS?

Elsie, a bilingual Puerto Rican woman in her late 20s, describes a transition meeting for one of her Latina students with a disability:

> A perfect example, one of my students, the parent doesn't know English, undocumented, but just a real nice person, comes always to all the meetings. But when we have the meeting, I don't know

if it's the fact that even though he knows me, he doesn't know everybody else involved, and this is a child who needs a lot of services, so there are a lot of people in our meetings. And I believe he feels like, you know, "What am I doing here?" He just stays really quiet, and when I ask him a direct question, that is the only time he participates. (Trainor, 2007, p. 97)

Elsie was a practicing high school special education teacher in Del Centro, a midwestern community in the United States with a high school population of 68% Latino (of Puerto Rican and Mexican heritage), the majority being Spanish speakers. Elsie was selected to serve as a community connector in a project designed to promote culturally responsive person-centered planning (PCP) in transition. She shared a cultural and linguistic background with some of the young adults with disabilities who participated in the project, resided in their community, and was acquainted with their families (Trainor, 2007). Her comments about a father feeling overwhelmed by the transactions that took place at the transition meeting for his child are indicative of the challenges faced by many CLD families of youth with disabilities in the transition planning process.

Lupe Espinosa's Transition Planning Meeting

Elizabeth Espinosa is a Latina woman in her mid-30s who emigrated to the United States from Mexico 5 years ago. She is the mother of a 16-year-old girl named Lupe, who has a moderate developmental disability. The transition IEP meeting at her daughter's high school begins promptly at 10:45 a.m. during the prep period of Lupe's special education teacher. Also in attendance are the school psychologist, an employment specialist for the district, a Spanish-speaking English language learner (ELL) teacher who will serve as translator, and an administrative designee. Lupe's service coordinator from the developmental disability center attends the meeting, as does Lupe herself.

The special education teacher begins by explaining to Mrs. Espinosa and Lupe that the primary purpose of the meeting is to plan for Lupe's remaining high school program and to discuss goals for Lupe's future. Mrs. Espinoza indicates her understanding. Further, she shares her efforts to teach Lupe tasks to help at home and in a family member's dress shop. The IEP team emphasizes other jobs in the community (fast food jobs) but Mrs. Espinoza balks. Her family needs Lupe's assistance at home. This meeting ends with the teacher asking for the parent's signature on the transition EIP. The teacher explains that a Spanish version will be mailed in two weeks. The parent signs the IEP.

The case study of Lupe Espinosa illustrates a number of challenges faced by CLD families of youth with disabilities in transition planning meetings. These include a lack of culturally responsive dialogue, a lack of understanding and respect for the family's culture, and a failure to acknowledge the family's hopes and dreams for their child's future. In fact, a body of literature exists on the lack of culturally responsive transition planning for CLD families of youth with disabilities. Table 1.3 contains a summary of the

Table 1.3. Themes in the literature and from focus groups with culturally and linguistically diverse families regarding transition for youth with disabilities

Theme	Supportive literature
Lack of understanding of our culture; our culture as a liability	Brandon and Brown (2009)
	Gil-Kashiwabara, Hogansen, Geenen, Powers, and Powers (2007)
	Harry (2008)
	Pewewardy and Fitzpatrick (2009)
	Rueda, Monzo, Shapiro, Gomez, and Blacher (2005)
Lack of respect for us and our children	Brandon and Brown (2009)
	Harry (2008)
	Lai and Ishiyama (2004)
	Rueda et al. (2005)
Lack of acknowledgment of our hopes and dreams for our child's future	Lai and Ishiyama (2004)
	Landmark, Zhang, and Montoya (2007)
	Pewewardy and Fitzpatrick (2009)
Lack of understanding of the legal requirements for transition	Rueda et al. (2005)
	Landmark et al. (2007)
	Povenmire-Kirk, Lindstrom, and Bullis (2010)
Racial and cultural stereotypes and biases of school professionals	Brandon and Brown (2009)
	Geenen, Powers, Lopez-Vasquez, and Bersani (2003)
	Gil-Kashiwabara et al. (2007)
	Harry (2008)
	Landmark et al. (2007)
Immigration issues, lack of language proficiency, and differences in cultural attitudes and norms affecting our views of transition for our youth	Geenen et al. (2003)
	Kochhar-Bryant and Greene (2009)
	Lai and Ishiyama (2004)
	Leake and Boone (2007)
	Olivos (2009)
	Povenmire-Kirk et al. (2010)
	Rueda et al. (2005)
	Trainor (2007)
Generational conflicts related to the transition to adult life	Kochhar-Bryant and Greene (2009)
	Leake and Boone (2007)

overall themes found in this literature. Table 1.4 contains implications for practitioners derived from these themes.

Lack of Understanding of Our Culture: Our Culture as a Liability

Rueda, Monzo, Shapiro, Gomez, and Blacher (2005) stated that the transition models, laws, and policies in this country assume that all parties involved in the collaborative process share corresponding values and goals about transition (e.g., goals focused on adult independent functioning and productivity). However, these authors noted that these assumptions do not hold up well in all cultures that make up American society. Findings from

Table 1.4. Implications for practice for interacting with culturally and linguistically diverse families of youth with disabilities in the transition planning process

1. Get to know a family's cultural background and beliefs when planning transition goals for their child.
2. Ask for, listen to, and respect parents' perspectives and what they have to say about their child with a disability.
3. Encourage parents to share their hopes and dreams for their child's future, even if they are different from your beliefs about the child. Support their hopes and dreams as much as possible by using them to help craft transition goals reflective of a positive future for the child and the family.
4. Provide families of youth with disabilities basic information about special education law related to transition in a form that is easy for them to understand.
5. Be sensitive to the basic survival needs of families (e.g., employment that cannot be interfered with) by scheduling meetings at a time and place that is convenient for them.
6. Be aware of attitudes about families when interacting with them in conferences and meetings. Always act professionally, and be willing to show empathy and sensitivity for their life circumstances.
7. Take the necessary time to build trust, rapport, and credibility with immigrant families of youth with disabilities to help ease potential fears of deportation.
8. Provide transition materials and discussions in a form that is easy for families to understand.
9. Keep an open mind because families may have different conceptions of individualism and independence and the importance of family and home.

focus group interviews with Latina mothers of children with disabilities demonstrated a "strong pattern of shared vision by these mothers; the overarching theme that emerged from the data was the mothers' view of transition as *home-centered, sheltered adaptation*, as opposed to a model emphasizing independent productivity" (Shapiro, Monzo, Rueda, Gomez, & Blacher, 2004, p. 406, as cited in Harry, 2008). This is clearly illustrated in the case study of Lupe Espinosa: Mrs. Espinosa's vision for Lupe was for her to live at home, help with family and child care needs, and work in a family-owned dress shop in the neighborhood. Adult independent functioning and productivity were not specific goals that Mrs. Espinosa had for Lupe in the distant future. Similarly, Pewewardy and Fitzpatrick (2009) pointed out that most American Indian families ultimately conceive of caring for and supporting children with disabilities as an expression of their native cultural beliefs. For example, they believe that disability is part of the spirit that inhabits the body rather than a defect. Their child is accepted by them and considered a member of their community. Therefore, they are reluctant to seek outside services for a child or to look for the child to leave the tribal community as he or she grows older. This is also true for Mrs. Espinosa, who did not want an employment specialist working with Lupe but rather wanted to have Lupe work in a family-owned business in the neighborhood. Moreover, Mrs. Espinosa was anxious about Lupe being exposed to strangers in the workplace. Rueda et al. reinforced these points by noting that although the special education system repeatedly tries to view the young adult child with a disability as an autonomous individual, for many Latina mothers of children with disabilities, this approach represents a "disturbing violation" of the views "of the child as embedded in the family" (p. 412). Clearly this applies to Mrs. Espinosa. Although in the transition meeting she often said, "I understand" when the special education professionals were presenting their plan designed to promote adult independence for Lupe, Mrs. Espinosa's words were hardly a ringing endorsement of this plan.

The transition models, laws, and policies in this country assume that all parties involved in the collaborative process share corresponding values and goals about transition (Rueda et al., 2005).

The theme of culture as a liability appears in a number of articles cited in Table 1.3. In a survey conducted by Gil-Kashiwabara, Hogansen, Geenen, Powers, and Powers, parents of Latina students with disabilities were more likely than parents of Anglo students with disabilities to endorse the statement "People expected less of her [my daughter] because of her race or culture" (2007, p. 85). One student quoted in the article mentioned the following about the way CLD students, including Latinas, are treated in school:

IMPLICATIONS FOR PRACTICE

Get to know a family's cultural background and beliefs when planning transition goals with their child. Create a list of postsecondary goals with the student and family.

> Many times at schools how you are treated depends on how the teachers are, and the teacher's opinion of the race. So, some teachers are very helpful in many ways, and some will kind of exclude you from the group if you're Latina or another race. (p. 85)

In Geenen, Powers, Lopez-Vasquez, and Bersani, the parent of an American Indian child with a disability described an incident that demonstrated disrespect and disregard for her child's culture:

> My daughter came home and said "I'm done. I'm not going back....This is crazy," and that one incident by itself was enough to get her out of school. She went to school and they were studying about the Iroquois....The teacher was teaching about the Iroquois and it was in the past tense. And she got mad, and then they broke up into small groups and one kid said "Why are we studying this? They're all dead anyway." And Laura said "Do I look dead to you?" and then she came home and she said that's it. I'm out. (2003, p. 36)

Additional examples of culture as a liability are offered by Harry (2008), who cited a study by Harry, Klinger, and Hart (2005) in which school personnel made "common sense" assumptions about appropriate family structures for three African American families living in poverty. The school personnel believed that because only five of the mother's nine children were living with her, the others must have been "farmed out somewhere," a demeaning, disrespectful phrase they used to imply that the mother did not care about her children and had abandoned them. In fact, the other four oldest children (i.e., those who were not living with the mother) were living with their paternal grandparents in another state.

"Deficit mothering" assumptions such as these were also illustrated in an ethnographic study by Lea (2006, as cited in Harry, 2008). A young African American mother who was getting private speech therapy for her son with a disability was quoted as saying that the service provider saw her as "just another Black girl who had a baby and not married....I know she look down on me but I just play the game....They don't know me. They don't know nothin' about me" (Lea, 2006, as cited in Harry, 2008, p. 376). Gil-Kashiwabara et al. mentioned that "many Latinas are stereotyped as caring more about marriage and childbearing than going to college; subsequently postsecondary education is not encouraged in their transition planning" (2007, p. 89). This false assumption is illustrated in the case study of Lupe Espinosa. Although Mrs. Espinosa wanted Lupe to help at home with the family, she also wanted her to someday take community college classes; however, Mrs. Espinosa was discouraged by the special education teacher who said that students such as Lupe usually are not successful in community college and need a more basic education to succeed in life.

A similar point was raised in an article by Brandon and Brown on ways to increase the involvement of African American families in the special education process:

> There appears to be a recursive cycle concerning the noninvolvement of African American parents in the school setting. Parents do not feel welcome, and educators believe that parents' lack of involvement signals apathy....School personnel must understand the barriers created within the school that might lead to negative perceptions and poor parental participation. (2009, p. 87)

These comments apply to many CLD families, including the Espinosas. Although Elizabeth was thanked at the end of the meeting for her participation, she could hardly be described as having been an active participant. Her several comments of "I understand" are possible indicators of her withdrawing from more active participation because of feeling unwelcome at the meeting.

A stereotype about many Latina mothers is that they care more about marriage and childbearing than going to college (Gil-Kashiwabara et al., 2007).

Lack of Respect for Us and Our Children

According to Brandon and Brown (2009), many African American parents of children with disabilities feel a sense of alienation and estrangement when interacting with education professionals because of a perceived lack of educator respect for them. Rueda et al. (2005), for example, noted that some of the Latina mothers in their focus groups believed that their involvement in the transition decision-making process was only "perfunctory" and that many professionals demonstrated an attitude of preferring that the mothers be less involved and less informed. Not providing work placement and transition information to the mothers in Spanish was offered as an example of this finding. Similarly, the case study of Lupe Espinosa demonstrates a lack of respect for the language differences of many members of the Latino community: The transition plan and information, although orally translated into Spanish, was not written in Spanish. Further, the family's suggestions were disregarded and the mother was urged to sign the transition IEP.

In the focus group of Chinese parents of youth and adults with disabilities interviewed for this book, the issue of a lack of respect from school personnel was evident in many comments. Participants mentioned that in their culture and community, parents want and are expected to help their child do everything that he or she is capable of doing. This includes parents being willing to spend extra time and money and cut other family expenses in order to help their child succeed. One parent even commented, "The child's outcome in life reflects on the parent's responsibility; we are their parents for their whole life, whether they are disabled or not!" Despite this perspective, the parents did not feel respected by the school personnel with whom they interacted during the transition planning process for their children. Comments made that exemplified this feeling included 1) "Chinese family expectations for our children include

"The child's outcome in life reflects on the parent's responsibility; we are their parents for their whole life, whether they are disabled or not!" (Chinese parent of a youth with a developmental disability)

academics, but they think this expectation is too high"; 2) "Sometimes we feel that we have to prove what our children can do"; 3) "If parents don't ask for certain things, they don't tell you"; and 4) "Schools should listen to what our hopes and dreams are for our children rather than assuming our child can't learn or do something; some children can learn on their own." A study published by Lai and Ishiyama (2004) on the involvement of Chinese Canadian mothers of children with disabilities yielded similar findings. The authors of this study offered the following observation:

> Although the value of education and devotion to the child drove the participants to be involved in their children's education, conflict resulted from differences of values and practices, the avoidance type of conflict resolution, and the language barrier moved the participants from active school involvement. (p. 104)

Harry (2008) reinforced many similar comments and findings in her review of the literature on collaboration with CLD families, noting that cross-cultural misunderstandings, assumptions of family impairments, and professionals' lack of awareness of their own biases often serve as obstacles to more active participation in special education of CLD families of children with disabilities.

IMPLICATIONS FOR PRACTICE

Use what you learn to inform your interactions with the student and his or her family.

Lack of Acknowledgment of Our Hopes and Dreams for Our Child's Future

In the case study of Lupe Espinosa, Mrs. Espinosa's hopes and dreams for her daughter's future are not acknowledged by the transition IEP team. Mrs. Espinosa wants Lupe to continue to live at home after completing high school, help with family responsibilities, and work part time in a neighborhood dress shop in order to contribute to the family's income, but the transition planning team has completely different ideas about what Lupe should be doing in the future. The team members include no input from Mrs. Espinosa, nor do they attempt to resolve Lupe's disconnected postsecondary goals. Landmark, Zhang, and Montoya commented about this in their article about CLD parents' experiences with their children's transition:

> Families of diverse cultures often value and emphasize a set of behaviors that are different from those valued and emphasized by the main culture. Many culturally diverse parents of students with disabilities may not always agree with the dominant Anglo-European culture's need for independence. (2007, p. 69)

They continued by noting that, as a result of this, some CLD parents feel more comfortable being involved in home-based transition activities, such as talking to their youth about post–high school life and teaching them cultural values and beliefs rather than being involved in school-based transition activities. These thoughts were echoed by Pewewardy and Fitzpatrick (2009), who cautioned that it is extremely important that educators working with American Indian families who have children with disabilities respect and support the families' cultural backgrounds because their belief system differs significantly from the views of mainstream U.S. society. The authors implied that American Indian cultures believe it is the tribe's responsibility to care for and support children with disabilities rather than for these individuals to seek future independence from their elders, tribe, and culture. This view of transition needs to be acknowledged, respected, and encouraged by school personnel when discussing transition with American Indian families in order to reduce potential cross-cultural conflicts or misunderstandings.

The notion of differing cultural perspectives on special education was illustrated in Lai and Ishiyama's (2004) study of Chinese Canadian immigrant mothers of children with disabilities. One mother tried to share her experiences and ideas with her son's teachers but was disappointed when the teachers showed no interest in hearing the educational practices of her home country. In the interviews of Chinese parents of youth and adults with disabilities conducted for this book, parents expressed concern that school transition personnel were less than willing to acknowledge the parents' desire for their children with moderate to severe disabilities to receive a traditional education that included academics rather than just a focus on life skills. Note that the Individuals with Disabilities Education Act (IDEA) of 1990 (PL 101-476) and its subsequent amendments require that all students with disabilities have access to the general education curriculum. These parents truly believed that their children could learn, wanted their children exposed to general education materials and technology and experiences with peers without disabilities, and wanted their children to be encouraged to reach academic goals as high as possible. This was not well received by school transition personnel, who demonstrated a lower set of expectations.

IMPLICATIONS FOR PRACTICE

Encourage families to share their hopes and dreams for their students' futures, even if they differ from your beliefs. Incorporate the family's comments, using them to craft meaningful postsecondary goals.

Lucius Washington's Transition IEP meeting

Thelma Washington, an African American woman in her mid-40s, is attending her 16-year-old son Lucius's transition planning meeting. Lucius has received special education services since second grade. He is currently in 11th grade, has a learning disability, and receives resource specialist program (RSP) services in reading, writing, and math. He functions at around a fifth- to sixth-grade level in most academic areas and requires ongoing RSP support in order to participate in general education classes. These supports include RSP tutoring, accommodations on assignments when appropriate, and alternative ways of demonstrating his learning. Lucius is required to complete the same curriculum as his peers without disabilities. Lucius attends a large, ethnically mixed inner-city high school in his neighborhood. He has attended local public schools in this district since kindergarten. Lucius has some friends whom he has known since elementary school. He lives with his mother and older sister, a senior in high school.

Lucius has been involved in recreational sports leagues since elementary school at the local Boys Club. He plays on the junior varsity basketball team at his high school and runs track in the spring. He also works part time at a coffee shop. His mother is active in her local church and attends regularly. She required Lucius and his sister to attend church until they turned 16. Because of their busy schedules with school, work, and activities, she now does not expect them to be in church regularly on Sundays.

The transition planning meeting is held after school and begins at 3:30 p.m. The transition individualized education program (IEP) team did not think this would be a problem because they assumed that Mrs. Washington would not be attending the meeting. In their experience, they have found that a lot of minority parents do not attend IEP meetings after their child completes elementary or middle school. Mrs. Washington works two jobs in the community, and although it is very difficult for her to make arrangements with her employers to take off work, she attends IEP meetings as often as possible. Her employers were aware of how important the meeting was to Mrs. Washington and granted her time off to attend. Lucius is also in attendance but can stay for only a short time because he does not want to miss basketball practice; he has a big game coming up this week and is a starter on the team. His RSP teacher is coordinating the meeting and in addition to her, the school psychologist, an employment specialist with the high school, an administrative designee, and a few of Lucius's general education teachers are present.

The meeting begins with introductions and a statement of the purpose of the meeting, which is to focus on creating a transition IEP for Lucius. Mrs. Washington says, "I know about an IEP, but what is a transition IEP? Nobody has ever explained this to me before." The RSP teacher explains what a transition IEP is and tells her that they will be discussing Lucius's academic program for his remaining time in high school and what he might like to do after high school. The RSP teacher says, "It's important for Lucius to tell us today what he might like his future to look like so we can try to make this happen for him. Special education law encourages students to engage in self-determination and setting their own transition goals." In addition, the RSP teacher tells Mrs. Washington that perhaps she is not aware that Lucius can sign for his own IEP when he turns 18. Mrs. Washington replies, "All right then, but don't I get to talk about the boy's future? I am his mother, you know." The RSP teacher reassures Mrs. Washington by saying, "Please understand, Mrs. Washington, that we are not trying to exclude you from the conversation taking place in this meeting. You will have a chance to share your thoughts about the transition goals for Lucius, and we welcome your input." Mrs. Washington responds, "Well, I appreciate that. I just don't know much about all of this legal stuff. Thank you for explaining it to me."

The two general education teachers in attendance subsequently present information about Lucius's academic progress in class, stating that he struggles with the curriculum but is able to keep up because he receives one period a day of RSP study skills support, which includes checking all of his homework assignments each day and providing him assistance as needed. They believe that with accommodations, Lucius will be able to pass the high school exit exam, receive his diploma, and possibly take classes at a community college in the future. Mrs. Washington expresses gratitude to the RSP teacher for "helping my boy in school." Lucius is then asked what he would like to do after high school, where he would like to live, and what kind of work he might like to do. Lucius says he is not sure what he would like to do after high school but that he does want to graduate with his friends and definitely go on to college because he is hoping he can play college basketball someday. He does not know if he can manage playing ball, working, and going to school, but he would like to give it a try.

"What type of work might you like to do, Lucius?" asks the employment specialist.

Lucius replies, "Maybe work in a sporting goods store, or athletic shoe store, or something like that."

The employment specialist says, "That's fine, Lucius, but those are low-paying jobs where you can't earn enough money to live on your own. What have you thought about in terms of a career?"

Lucius replies, "It'd be cool if I could make it into the NBA!" The employment specialist mentions that very few college players make it into the NBA and encourages Lucius to have an alternative career plan just in case he does not play professional basketball.

Lucius replies, "Something to do with sports, I guess. Maybe coaching or working at the Boys Club someday. I loved that place when I was a little kid."

The employment specialist responds, "Sounds like you have some ideas to look into as we get you involved in career exploration activities in the next few years. Would you agree?" Lucius nods his head in agreement. Lucius's RSP teacher then asks him where he would like to live after completing high school. He says, "Man, I would like to get out of this neighborhood and live uptown somewhere. But for a while, I think I'll live at home if I go to community college." The RSP teacher says that she will explore with Lucius various living options and costs in his senior year in high school.

Attention now turns to Mrs. Washington. The RSP teacher asks her for her thoughts on all of these things. Mrs. Washington begins by saying, "I had no idea that we were going to be talking about these things today. I thought this was just another one of those IEP meetings. If I had known about this I would have talked these things over with Lucius at home before we came to this meeting."

The RSP teacher apologizes to Mrs. Washington and says that "the team meant no disrespect."

Mrs. Washington says, "Fine then. I'll give you my thoughts. I want Lucius to get his diploma because it's damn hard to make much of yourself in this world without one. I also would like to see him go on to college, but I'm worried about college classes. He struggles now in his high school classes. As for working and living on his own, maybe someday, but if he isn't living at home, what's going to happen to my benefits? If I lose those benefits, then I'm going to need his help to get by for a while. I'm working two jobs right now just to make ends meet. So maybe just for a little while he can live with me while he starts college, keeps working like he is now, and then gradually get off on his own. That would help me a lot." The administrative designee says that he has heard this concern expressed before, and although he sympathizes with Mrs. Washington's situation, he thinks it is important someday in the future "for Lucius to break this cycle of dependency and get out on his own and start his own life." Lucius reassures his mom that he will always try to help take care of her in any way he can. Mrs. Washington gives Lucius an affectionate pat on the hand.

The meeting ends with writing the transition plan goals and designating service providers who will offer support for Lucius. These include the employment specialist, the representative at the Office of Disabled Student Services at the local community college, the high school employment specialist, and the high school resource specialist throughout high school.

Lack of Understanding of the Legal Requirements for Transition

The case study of Lucius Washington is indicative of one of the primary problems faced by many CLD families of youth with disabilities. Some CLD families lack knowledge and understanding of the legal requirements of transition and their role in the process (Kochhar-Bryant & Greene, 2009; Landmark et al., 2007; Salembier & Furney, 1997). This is clearly evident in the comments of Mrs. Washington. She did not know what a transition IEP meant, was unaware that special education law encouraged youth with disabilities to engage in self-determination and advocacy regarding planning for their future, and did not know that a youth with a disability could legally sign for his or her own IEP at age 18, the age of majority.

Many CLD families lack knowledge and understanding of special education law related to transition and do not know their own or their child's role in the process.

Lack of parent knowledge and understanding of transition-related laws is evident in several publications (Gil-Kashiwabara et al., 2007; Landmark et al., 2007; Rueda et al., 2005; Wehman, 2006). Latina mothers of young adults with developmental disabilities in the transition study conducted by Rueda et al. felt that they lacked information regarding transition planning and services. Some of the parents in this study believed that this was intentional on the part of special education personnel, as evidenced by one parent's comment about the negative consequences of becoming educated about transition service requirements: "When a parent starts getting too smart and really learning the system then you little by little become a persona non grata wherever you go because you know the system, you know your rights and they like resent it" (p. 408).

Landmark et al.'s (2007) study of the experiences of CLD parents in their child's transition found that parents had minimal knowledge of the legal requirements of transition. For example, 37% of the parents in their study said that they did not know what transition planning was, and 16% stated that they knew little to nothing about their child's transition planning. Moreover, "overwhelmingly, those parents who responded that they were not familiar with the phrase *transition planning* were culturally diverse" (p. 72). One mother in the study said the following about the transition planning process for her child: "We really don't know what may be the next step" (p. 72). The Chinese parents of youth and adults with developmental disabilities interviewed for this book also mentioned a lack of information about transition. Comments made included "I was not given much information"; "I needed to know more about the options for my child's future"; "I had to do a lot of things on my own"; "There was not good planning, connection, or follow-through with services for my child"; and "The options offered were not based on my child's needs." Finally, a study by Povenmire-Kirk, Lindstrom, and Bullis (2010) sought to identify and describe the transition needs of Latino youth with disabilities and obtained results similar to those of previous published literature on this topic. Latino families interviewed by Povenmire-Kirk et al. reported not having enough information or understanding about transition, their roles in the process, or opportunities for participation. The parents in this study further reported that they did not know where to obtain such information about

IMPLICATIONS FOR PRACTICE

Provide families of youth with disabilities basic information about special education law related to transition in a form that is easy for them to understand. Create a checklist for parents targeting required transition milestones.

their child or the responsibilities of the school with respect to transition. One parent's comments nicely summarized the issue of CLD parents' lack of understanding of the legal requirements related to youth with disabilities with regard to transition:

> I need more information. I mean, I'm getting all this information from [the multicultural liaison], but what happens when I leave? Where am I going to go? Who am I going to ask?...We need someone to help us understand when we need to be involved and to help the school understand that we work during the day. Some of us work at night too. (2010, p. 47)

Racial and Cultural Stereotypes and Biases of School Professionals

There are numerous examples in the literature of the racial and cultural stereotypes and biases of school professionals interacting with CLD families of youth with disabilities. A survey by Geenen et al. (2003) of minority parents of youth with disabilities who were involved in transition revealed that a significant number of parents reported that they did not feel that people in the schools showed respect for their child's race, nationality, or cultural background. Two direct quotes from Geenen et al. are representative of this finding: "When—when you take your kids to get certain services there's a certain—I don't want to say it, underlying racism" (p. 36), and "Our kids just get tagged as not able, because they're kids of color" (p. 36). An example of a cultural stereotype in the case study of Lucius Washington is the transition IEP team scheduling the meeting to take place at 3:30 p.m. on a school day because it is assumed that the mother will not attend. The fact that the scheduled meeting time significantly interfered with the mother's work schedule and two jobs also shows the team's disregard for her SES and basic survival needs. Landmark et al. (2007) reinforced this point by observing that the everyday struggles of providing for their families seemed to preclude many minority families in their study from participating at higher levels in their children's transition. The team showed further disrespect for Mrs. Washington by not explaining to her the purpose of the meeting in advance; she thought she was attending an ordinary IEP meeting and was not prepared to discuss Lucius's transition. A quote from a parent of a minority child with a disability further illustrates the point of cultural stereotypes and biases by school professionals: "I think the biggest thing is the insensitivity they [professionals] have around the needs of our minority families. They just don't get that we might possibly see the world differently than they do" (Geenen et al., 2003, p. 36).

Minority parents of youth with disabilities involved in transition reported that they often encountered insensitivity and discrimination in their encounters with school personnel (Geenen et al., 2003).

In discussing the perceptions of and reasons for noninvolvement of African American parents and families in special education, Brandon and Brown (2009) stated that two of the biggest concerns of African American parents about working with schools were 1) educator respect for them and their children and 2) negativity expressed by schools toward them and their children. The school administrative designee demonstrated such insensitivity and disrespect when Mrs. Washington mentioned her concern about finances; the designee responded, "It's important for Lucius to break this cycle." Cultural insensitivity and discrimination "was described as one of the most formidable barriers" by minority parents in the transition study conducted by Geenen et al. (2003, p. 36). The authors noted that this problem was repeatedly encountered by CLD parents of youth with disabilities on an individual level in everyday interactions with professionals, as well as throughout the system, in which parents experienced institutionally based inequities and discrimination. In addition, families reported in certain instances feeling intentionally punished or treated poorly by professionals because of their culture. Parent quotes reflecting these problems, as cited in Geenen et al., included the following: "My thing I always tell Dion, they'll [professionals] always judge you on how you look, how you speak…just because you're black…and sometimes I hate to emphasize that, but it's a reality, you know, and it hurts" (p. 36), and "I think if you have to deal with the racism and you have to deal with the stigma that goes with some kind of difference of having a disability, it is really difficult" (p. 36).

IMPLICATIONS FOR PRACTICE

Be sensitive to the basic survival needs of families (e.g., employment that cannot be interfered with) by scheduling meetings at a time and place that is convenient for them.

Other examples of cultural biases, or "cross cultural misunderstandings," as Harry (2008, p. 377) referred to them, in the CLD transition literature come from Gil-Kashiwabara et al. (2007). Their survey found that, compared with Anglo parents of students with disabilities, more Latina mothers of students in special education reported school personnel having lower expectations for their child based on the child's race or culture. Moreover, in focus groups Latina students with disabilities reported the negative impact of ethnic and racial stereotypes they had experienced in classes with certain teachers. As mentioned previously, the authors noted that many Latinas with disabilities are not encouraged in their transition planning meetings to pursue postsecondary education because they are stereotyped as caring more about marriage and childbearing than going to college. And yet the results of Gil-Kashiwabara et al. revealed the high importance and value placed on education by Latina families (i.e., 63% of Latina parents surveyed said it was "very important" for their daughters with disabilities to attend college in the next 5 years compared with 34% of Anglo parents of girls with disabilities). Two parents in a focus group conducted by Gil-Kashiwabara et al. poignantly illustrate the inaccuracy of this stereotype of Latinas:

IMPLICATIONS FOR PRACTICE

Be aware of your attitudes about families when interacting with them in conferences and meetings. Always act professionally, and be willing to show empathy and sensitivity for their life circumstances.

> At the university we hear that there are lots of obstacles, like it's very expensive, but I tell her that if she gets accepted to university…she will have all of my support and everything I can do for her. It's important to me as a parent to have my child in a university. (p. 84)

> If my daughter has a child, I would help her in any way I could (to go to school)…and I tell her that she needs to move forward and she doesn't need to do the same thing that I'm doing….God willing she doesn't end up pregnant and having a child, but if she does, I will support her. (p. 84)

Immigration Issues, Lack of Language Proficiency, and Differences in Cultural Attitudes and Norms Affecting Our Views of Transition for Our Youth

Olivos (2009) noted that the dramatic increase in the Latino population, both documented and undocumented, in the United States since the mid-1990s has resulted in state and federal policy makers responding with increased enforcement measures aimed at curbing undocumented immigration. This has had clear consequences for school personnel, including those in special education, because immigrant families with undocumented heads of household do not want to draw unnecessary attention from government employees. This can result in Latino families not going to school to talk with IEP teams or avoiding filling out paperwork that requires them to provide personal information. Olivos pointed out that "Latino parents tend to view educators as government employees who are thus accountable for enforcing federal immigration" (p. 112). Likewise, a special education teacher involved in transition planning with Latino families stated, "Families that are undocumented and have had negative experiences think that if they get involved in one thing or the other, it puts them at risk for being deported" (Trainor, 2007, p. 98). Povenmire-Kirk et al. (2010) stated that concerns around documentation create trust issues and logistical barriers for school personnel that influence the type of transition services they can deliver to CLD youth with disabilities. Their study of Latino families of youth with disabilities found that "school staff members often struggled with trying to open lines of communication with students who feared that their families might be deported or worse" (p. 45).

IMPLICATIONS FOR PRACTICE

Take the necessary time to build trust, rapport, and credibility with immigrant families of youth with disabilities to help ease potential fears of deportation, and create a safe environment.

Finally, a different type of discomfort related to immigration was discussed by Lai and Ishiyama. The Chinese immigrant mothers in their study reported experiencing various degrees of stress related to relocating from China to Canada and adapting to the Canadian culture. This was particularly difficult for three mothers who had been in Canada for only a short period of time, who lacked English proficiency, and whose children with disabilities were approaching adulthood. One of the mothers in the study said, "Coming here, all I see is a cloud of dust....Did we make a wrong choice? It is like a big drop off for me" (2004, p. 102).

The literature reports that limited English proficiency is a common reason why many CLD families do not actively participate in the special education and transition planning process. Families who do not speak or understand English well are at a distinct disadvantage when interacting with school professionals during transition planning meetings. In the transition study conducted by Rueda et al. (2005), Latina mothers noted a lack of viable sources of transition-related information in Spanish (e.g., work placements and other transition services). Moreover, the mothers pointed out that even translating written transition materials into Spanish did not remove all barriers because many of the immigrant mothers lacked sufficient reading skills to comprehend the complex transition language used. Trainor (2007) offered further evidence of the problems immigrant Latino parents experience in transition meetings as a result of their lacking sufficient English literacy and language skills. Elsie, a Spanish-speaking classroom teacher who participated as a community liaison in the study, was trained to use PCP in transition with Spanish-speaking families of youth with disabilities in her community. Elsie was quoted as saying the following:

Families who do not speak or understand English well are at a distinct disadvantage when interacting with school professionals during transition planning meetings. Work with an interpreter to allow the family better understanding of the information being presented at the meeting.

I do have a couple of parents who don't know how to read and whose English is very limited. And I do spend so much time translating back and forth in a traditional IEP meeting that when it's time, my kids [those from her classroom] are already coming in the classroom, and they're [the parents] so nice about it…they just say, "Okay, I trust you." That's not what you want to foster in parents. It's nice that they trust you, but you want to foster their involvement and questioning because that's how we get to where we want to get. (p. 98)

This quote represents another common cause of cultural bumps, specifically deference to authority in transition planning meetings. In their study of Chinese Canadian immigrant mothers of children with disabilities, Lai and Ishiyama noted that similar to parents in Asian countries, many of the mothers in their study "continued to place themselves one rung below the teachers after immigration, both out of respect for the authority figures and as experts in their field" (2004, p. 104). This often resulted in the mothers listening to the teachers rather than taking an active role in parent–teacher communication or openly expressing their needs and concerns regarding their children with disabilities. A staff member talking about a school's perceived lack of involvement of Latino parents in transition planning meetings demonstrates CLD parents' respect for teachers and how school personnel misinterpret parents' motives:

IMPLICATIONS FOR PRACTICE

Provide transition materials and discussions in a form that is easy for minority families to understand.

There is nothing in a school for a Latino family that is more respectable than a teacher. And when parents don't speak—when they look at the teacher and nod, it doesn't mean that they're being disrespectful or that they have no questions. It means that they're feeling belittled because they're not understanding what the teacher is saying because they [the parents] didn't have the education or they had first or second grade education and they feel they can't intelligently enough say what they have to say. (Povenmire-Kirk et al., 2010, p. 47)

Differences in cultural attitudes and norms can have a profound effect on CLD family participation in the transition planning process. Special education law encourages the active participation and advocacy of parents when exploring outcomes for their child's future. And yet, many CLD families do not feel comfortable in this role because of cultural differences between them and the individuals with whom they are interacting. Kochhar-Bryant and Greene pointed out that members of different cultures respond differently to having a child with a disability: "In some nations [Russia for example], children with disabilities are hidden and not presented as part of the family" (2009, p. 444). In contrast, the common belief among Native Americans is that the spirit chooses the body that it will inhabit; a body with a disability is merely the outward casing of the spirit, which is whole and perfect (Clay, 2007; Locust, 1988, 1994).

Two other common causes of cultural bumps CLD families of youth with disabilities exhibit in transition planning meetings are family as value and deference to authority.

Finally, Kochhar-Bryant and Greene reported that many African Americans have a history of experiences with and concerns about their children being misdiagnosed as having a mild disability or being misplaced in special education classes, resulting in lower expectations for their children among school personnel. A quote from an African American parent in the transition study conducted by Geenen et al. illustrates this concern: "I know what you mean about the labels, because they had my daughter in special ed. And I told them [school staff] look, just because Dion has a lot of internal medical problems, there's nothing wrong with her mind" (2003, p. 39).

Another norm common to several cultural groups is family as value. Leake and Boone (2007) studied multicultural perspectives on self-determination, considered a key aspect of transition planning for youth with disabilities. They found that varying cultural conceptions of *family* significantly influenced the self-determination of youth with disabilities and that a CLD conception of family tended to be much broader than that of the stereotypical nuclear family in the United States. For example, a White teacher in Hawaii made the following comments with respect to family as value:

> If you ask any of these students [in Hawaii] what's important to you, the first thing they say is their family connection. With the students in other places, that comes later in life. Back on the mainland, yeah, my family was important, but as a teenager, I was focusing on what I want. Here, the teenagers already have that connection with being part of a family and needing to do things because of that involvement. (p. 109)

Similar results were found in the study of Latina mothers by Rueda et al. (2005). The importance of the family and home versus individualism and independence was evident in the views of the mothers when discussing the futures of their daughters with disabilities. "Mothers' expectations, even for their nondisabled offspring, did not favor independent living arrangements without clearly sanctioned transition points such as marriage" (p. 409). Finally, the issue of cultural perceptions of disability in the context of family as value is clearly evident in the following quote from Trainor's study investigating CLD perspectives of transition:

> The kid [Latino] expressed that…family was really important to him, and he really wanted to eventually meet a nice girl, fall in love, get married, have kids, and move out. And it became clear to us that the family had not even thought about that. And they were upset because they wanted the kid to understand that, well, according to them, he could never do that. They really couldn't see him leaving the home, and I think culture did play a role in that situation, not, I mean, disability as well, but culturally they saw him still as a child. And they can't really see somebody leaving the house, especially if you're not married. (2007, p. 98)

IMPLICATIONS FOR PRACTICE

Keep an open mind, as families may have different conceptions of individualism and independence and the importance of family and home.

Generational Conflicts Related to the Transition to Adult Life

Kochhar-Bryant and Greene (2009) discussed the problems faced by CLD families of youth with disabilities with regard to generational conflicts. They reviewed the *cultural mismatch theory* (Delpit, 1995), which posits that "individuals who are culturally different from the majority population face challenges bridging the gap between the home and school cultures" (p. 426). Acculturation of second- and third-generation CLD youth with disabilities can result in differences in styles, values, beliefs, and understandings that lead to intergenerational conflicts. In the context of transition planning, this can become evident when CLD youth with disabilities are asked by school personnel to engage in self-determination, resulting in direct conflict with their parents' cultural values and beliefs. This problem is illustrated in several cases in Leake and Boone (2007), who studied multicultural perspectives on self-determination in CLD families of youth with disabilities. For example, a young native Hawaiian woman reported that her father's goal for her was not college: "He wanted me to actually stay at home and baby-sit all day…and I told him, I'm not gonna waste my time doing that" (p. 110). In another instance, a young Vietnamese man reported experiencing generational conflict over wanting to choose his own career; his father embraced "the family first orientation": "Like my dad, he's like straight up, like 2 years ago I told him I wanted to be a writer and an actor. He's like, 'F___ you. You're gonna live for yourself? F___ you,' and he hung up" (p. 111). Finally, quotes from a Filipino mother and her adult daughter demonstrate the intergenerational conflicts that can result when CLD youth with disabilities are encouraged to engage in self-determination regarding their futures.

> Daughter: In my growing up, self-determination, to me, meant moving out of the house. I wasn't an adult until I moved out.

> Mother: My daughter moved away, she left with her friend at age 23. She left me, basically. My son told me, "Mom, you told us we were going to have to take care of yourselves. Now she's doing that. Just let her." (p. 111)

SUMMARY

CLD families of youth with disabilities typically face additional challenges in the transition planning process beyond the challenge of disability alone. A lack of in-depth knowledge and understanding of the home culture by school personnel is a common problem noted in the literature. Differences in values, practices, and beliefs create cultural bumps when CLD families interact with school personnel while discussing their child's future. These can be exacerbated when school professionals demonstrate a lack of respect, disregard, or in some instances prejudice toward CLD families. Many CLD families are at a further disadvantage because of their lack of English language proficiency and their limited understanding of special education law related to transition. Minority families who have low SES face additional challenges that prevent them from being more actively involved in the transition planning process for their children. Their basic survival needs are often not taken into account by school personnel when scheduling and planning meetings or discussing transition matters during meetings. Immigration-related issues such as risk and fear of interacting with government employees because of immigration status can interfere with the open communication process intended to take place at a transition planning meeting. Another potential communication barrier is deference to authority, which can be misinterpreted by school personnel as lack of parent interest and active involvement in transition planning. Finally, the acculturation of youth with disabilities to the mainstream culture can result in intergenerational conflict within CLD families, for example when discussing goals for the child's future.

A number of implications for practice are interspersed throughout this chapter and summarized in Table 1.4. The focus of the rest of the book is further development of these implications; review of the literature on culturally responsive collaboration; and discussion of specific methods, materials, and resources for school personnel involved in transition planning with CLD families of youth with disabilities. It is hoped that the content presented here provides a basic foundation upon which to build better practice in terms of interacting with CLD families of youth with disabilities during the transition years.

2

Culturally Responsive Transition Planning and Recommended Practices

Common sense and ordinary human decency are at the heart of positive partnerships between families and professionals serving children with disabilities.

—M. Blue-Banning, J.A. Summers, H.C. Frankland, L.L. Nelson, and G. Beegle (2004, p. 181)

Planning for transition from school to a quality adult life for a youth with a disability is an extremely complex process involving multiple domains, individuals, and agencies. Parents and youth with disabilities play a critical role in the development of a transition IEP. However, the vast majority of parents of youth with disabilities report feeling ill-equipped to effectively participate in transition planning meetings (Kochhar-Bryant & Greene, 2009; Salembier & Furney, 1997). Wittig (2009) stressed that shifting the paradigm from teacher-developed goals to student-driven plans for the future is essential.

The challenge of promoting the active participation of parents and youth with disabilities in the transition process becomes exponentially greater when these individuals come from CLD backgrounds. Differences in cultural values and beliefs, life priorities, primary language, and day-to-day basic survival needs, along with many other challenges faced by CLD families of youth with disabilities, make it more difficult for CLD families to play an active role in transition planning. With this in mind, this chapter addresses the following questions:

1. What are the key elements and skills involved in culturally responsive collaboration in special education?
2. What are recommended practices in culturally responsive transition planning with CLD families of youth with disabilities, and what do these look like in public schools?

This chapter answers these important questions. Here I share case studies, implementation strategies, and suggestions along with published resources and materials to demonstrate how special education and transition personnel can apply recommended practices in real-world settings.

WHAT ARE THE KEY ELEMENTS AND SKILLS INVOLVED IN CULTURALLY RESPONSIVE COLLABORATION IN SPECIAL EDUCATION?

Harry (2008) offered a comprehensive review of research-based definitions and recommendations of ideal collaborative relationships between special education professionals and CLD families of youth with disabilities. Harry emphasized the importance of developing strong professional partnerships with CLD parents through the development of mutual trust and culturally sensitive communication. She cautioned professionals to avoid adopting deficit views of families and cross-cultural conflicts in setting goals for transition and to be aware of culturally based views of caregivers' roles that exist in other cultures. Blue-Banning et al. (2004) conducted 34 focus groups and 18 face-to-face interviews across 137 families who varied in age, SES, and ethnicity (i.e., 41% African American, 17% Latino, 30% White, and 4% other). Six central characteristics of effective collaboration emerged from this study (see Table 2.1). Including these in collaborations with CLD families does not require large investments in new resources because the characteristics are based on common sense and ordinary human decency and form the heart of positive partnerships between families and professionals serving children with disabilities (Blue-Banning et al., 2004). Harry (2008) cautioned, however, that "common sense and ordinary human decency" can be considered culturally bound constructs based on a particular view of reality and set of assumptions. "Human decency may be interpreted differently according to cultural and/or historic lenses" (Harry, 2008, p. 376). Although this may be true, I believe that in the vast majority of instances, special education professionals who keep these six characteristics in mind when interacting with CLD families of youth with disabilities will greatly increase the probability of achieving positive collaborative relationships.

In earlier work, Harry (1992) explored cultural diversity, families, and the special education system and offered further insight into ways to form positive relationships with CLD families of youth with disabilities. A key finding of this research was that an unequal balance of power exists between special education professionals and the families they serve; specifically, CLD families lack equal power in their typical interactions with special educators in the public school (e.g., during

An unequal balance of power exists between special education professionals and the CLD families they serve. This places CLD families at a distinct disadvantage when dealing with the school system (Harry, 1992).

teacher conferences, transition meetings). Harry noted that "the only consistent role offered to parents was that of consent-giver, and that the legalistic framing of this role tended to

Table 2.1.   Essential characteristics of effective collaboration

1. Communication that is positive, understandable, and respectful
2. Commitment to the child and family
3. Equal power in decision making and service implementation
4. Competence in implementing and achieving goals
5. Mutual trust
6. Mutual respect

Source: Blue-Banning, Summers, Frankland, Nelson, and Beegle (2004).

convert the notion of consent into a meaningless ritual of compliance" (1992, p. 239). She argued that this places CLD parents at a distinct disadvantage when dealing with school systems. Table 2.2 presents several alternative roles that CLD parents of youth with disabilities can take on as a way to create a more equal balance of power in special education collaboration. An example of these roles in practice can be found in the case study of Wen Lee.

Wen Lee's
Upcoming IEP Meeting

Mi Lee, a Chinese woman, is the mother of Wen, a ninth-grade child with a moderate intellectual disability. The Lee family lives and works in San Francisco, California, which has a large Chinese population. Wen has received special education services in the San Francisco Unified School District since preschool and functions in the low average range cognitively. He is enrolled full time in special education classes, has limited language and communication skills, and uses a Picture Exchange Communication System to express many of his needs. He is able to speak some words in English. His primary language is Chinese, and his family speaks Chinese in the home and community.

The special education team at his high school began the transition planning process with his family shortly after the start of the school year. The team has been trained in cultural reciprocity and as a result has implemented several procedures to make the process of communicating with the Lee family one that reflects cultural sensitivity. For example, they use a Chinese translator named Sue Wong. Ms. Wong is employed by the school district, is familiar with the local Chinese cultural community and customs and with special education law, and is able to provide needed supports to Chinese families of youth with disabilities. Ms. Wong recently visited the Lee home and was instrumental in getting a complete background from the Lee family regarding Wen's development, learning, and behavior; the type of high school program the family wished for him to receive in the coming years; and the family's preliminary thoughts about goals for Wen after he completes high school. Ms. Wong asked the Lees whether they would be comfortable

Table 2.2. Roles for parents of CLD youth with disabilities in special education

1. *Parents as assessors:* asking CLD parents to be included in the entire assessment process, with professionals relying on parents' intimate knowledge, cultural background, and experience with their own children to help provide key information
2. *Parents as presenters of reports:* expecting CLD parents to be present at conferences and meetings in order to give oral or written information that is considered valuable and essential to the creation of an official document such as an IEP or transition IEP
3. *Parents as policy makers:* allowing CLD parents to elect their own representatives to local school building or neighborhood advisory committees, resulting in 1) an increase in parents' responsibility and input into special education programming decision making and 2) their ability to express cultural or community concerns
4. *Parents as advocates and peer supports:* providing CLD parents with opportunities within schools to provide peer advocacy, provide support at IEP meetings, and serve as interpreters between the cultures of their community and the culture of the school

Source: Harry (1992).

Key: CLD, culturally and linguistically diverse; IEP, individualized education program.

sharing this information with the special education team in an upcoming IEP meeting. She assured them that she would attend the meeting and act as a translator on their behalf. She then shared with the Lees the documents that would be used in the meeting, which had been translated into Chinese for the Lee family to review. Ms. Wong also answered any questions the family had and addressed whatever concerns she could prior to the meeting.

The Lees said that they would be willing and able to present the report from the home meeting at the upcoming transition IEP meeting and that they appreciated the opportunity to have their thoughts and views reflected in the report. However, they did not feel entirely comfortable advocating for Wen in the meeting because they did not want to show any disrespect to the professionals working with their son. Ms. Wong said that she understood this concern and that other members of the Chinese community whose children were in special education had expressed similar concerns in the past. Ms. Wong asked the Lees whether they were familiar with or had had contact with the Chinese parent special education support group offered by the school district and whether they would be interested in talking to any of these parents. The Lees asked for the names of some of the parents in the group and when Ms. Wong shared some, the Lees smiled, because several of them were parents of other students in Wen's special education class. The Lees said that they would like to talk with some of these parents and hear about their experiences so that the process might be easier. Ms. Wong said that she would arrange for this to take place in a mutually comfortable setting and at a time that was convenient for all of the parents involved.

The home visit from Ms. Wong ended with the Lees feeling much better about the upcoming transition IEP meeting and thanking Ms. Wong for coming. They said that they looked forward to seeing her at the meeting. Ms. Wong said that she would be in touch with them soon to connect them with the parents they knew from the support group.

This case study highlights many of the roles for CLD parents of youth with disabilities in special education recommended by Harry (1992) and shown in Table 2.2. For example, the home visit Ms. Wong conducted offered the Lees the opportunity to be included in the transition process for the upcoming IEP meeting. They were asked to provide a comprehensive background about their son Wen and share their thoughts on his upcoming high school program and postsecondary goals after completing high school. Ms. Wong was able to get the Lees to agree to act as presenters of a report at the upcoming IEP meeting and told them that she would act as a translator at the meeting to help support them and make them feel comfortable. A final support Ms. Wong offered was the opportunity for the Lees to meet with parents of the Chinese parent special education support group. This was in response to the Lees' concern of not wanting to show disrespect to the special education professionals at the upcoming IEP meeting and wanting to know how to respectfully advocate for their child. The existence of this group is reflective of parents as policy makers, another recommended role for CLD parents.

Assessor, presenter of reports, policy maker, and advocate are all recommended roles for CLD parents of youth with disabilities in special education.

Lynch and Hanson (2004) identified five aspects of cultural competence that can optimize communication and interactions with CLD families of youth with disabilities:

1. An awareness of one's own cultural limitations
2. Openness, appreciation, and respect for cultural differences
3. A view of intercultural interactions as learning opportunities
4. The ability to use cultural resources in interventions
5. Acknowledgment of the integrity and value of all cultures

For example, a special educator who acknowledges that he or she does not speak the home language of the CLD parents attending an IEP meeting is aware of his or her own cultural limitations. Rather than assuming that the parents understand English, the IEP team should know far in advance of any meetings if the parents speak or understand English.

The following questions, which an IEP team should ask prior to an IEP/transition IEP meeting, represent culturally responsive collaboration with CLD families of youth with disabilities. These questions and others can be found in the chapter appendix.

1. Do you understand and read English, or would you like us to provide an interpreter at the meeting and written information in your home language?
2. How do your family and cultural community view the role of education in your child's life?
3. How does your family and cultural community feel about children with disabilities?
4. What resources are available within your family and in your cultural community that you might consider using to help your child with a disability?
5. All of us have thoughts and ideas about what is best for your child, but we would really like to hear your thoughts today. What do you think your child needs?
6. Is there anything we should know about your family or cultural community that can help us provide the best education possible for your child?
7. We consider your family and cultural background to be very important and want to show respect to you in discussing your child's education and future; what do you envision your child's future to look like?

These questions are examples of what Barrera and Corso (2003) referred to as "skilled dialogue." These authors suggested that "cultural diversity is a dynamic relation reality that exists *between* persons rather than within any single person" and that "cultural diversity is primarily based in relationship and communication issues (i.e., related to the challenges of dialogues across particular kinds of differences rather than cognitive issues fueled by knowledge or lack thereof)" (p. 36). Skilled dialogue is a *process* that reflects one's ability to interact with and form relationships with particular culture(s) that are respectful, reciprocal, and *responsive*. It is not based on the amount of information special educators have regarding particular cultures. Skilled dialogue honors both the individual uniqueness of a CLD family and its place in its larger culture.

Skilled dialogue is a process that reflects one's ability to interact with and form relationships with particular culture(s) that are respectful, reciprocal, and responsive (Barrera & Corso, 2003).

Consider respect, reciprocity, and responsiveness. Barrera and Corso noted that *respect* is a "hallmark of skilled dialogue" and "refers to an acknowledgment and acceptance of boundaries that exist between persons" (2003, p. 43). Such boundaries can be cognitive (e.g., what one believes to be true), emotional (e.g., words and actions that convey insult or praise), or spiritual (e.g., God, spirit, energy, self). People engaged in skilled dialogue demonstrate respect toward others by being willing to acknowledge differences in perceptions and boundaries as well as being able to suspend the need to make them match. An example of respect might be a special education professional acknowledging a CLD parent's different perception of his or her youth with a disability but seeking to achieve common ground in planning for the youth's future.

Reciprocity "builds on respect and seeks to balance power between persons in dialogue" (Barrera & Corso, 2003, p. 45). It offers each person in an interaction equal power, assumes equal capability, and demonstrates that each person is equally valued. It does not, however, deny the fact that one person in the collaborative process may possess more expertise, knowledge, or authority in a particular area (e.g., a transition specialist knows about various transition agencies and services that can be utilized to help a CLD youth with a disability find employment). Reciprocal interactions permit each person an opportunity to contribute to the discussion and to make choices with respect to the outcomes to be achieved. An example of reciprocity in a transition planning meeting at which the family and youth with a disability are present is a special educator saying, "I have my thoughts on what might be good goals for your future, but I am eager to hear what goals you and your family have. I hope today that we can all come to an agreement on what might be best to include in the transition IEP."

Finally, *responsiveness* refers to professionals "taking the next step" in skilled dialogue by allowing CLD families and youth with disabilities to "uncover who they are rather than shaping them into who we want or need them to be" (Remen, 2000, p. 281). An example of responsiveness on the part of professionals is a willingness to entertain other possibilities or to acknowledge that they do not have all of the answers in a collaborative interaction with a CLD family. Using phrases such as "I wonder if" or "Maybe" instead of "I know" or "I'm sure" are ways professionals can acknowledge not knowing exactly what to do or say when engaged in skilled dialogue (Barrera & Corso, 2003, p. 47).

Leake and Black (2005) emphasized the importance of cultural reciprocity when they discussed how to provide culturally sensitive individualized transition services and supports to CLD families of youth with disabilities. The authors cited the work of Kalyanpur and Harry (1997, 1999), who wrote in depth on the concept of cultural reciprocity. The use of cultural reciprocity is a general means of enhancing relationships with all families, not just CLD families. A key aspect of cultural reciprocity is becoming aware of the cultural assumptions that guide one's thinking and behavior. This in turn makes it possible for an individual to be sensitive to cultural differences.

The posture of cultural reciprocity involves five key features:

1. Going beyond an awareness of differences to an awareness of self
2. Aiming to be aware of more subtle levels of difference versus those that are surface level or stereotypic
3. Applying awareness universally so that families and personnel are able to communicate, collaborate, listen, respect, and respond to all perspectives
4. Avoiding stereotypical solutions or a one-size-fits-all perspective
5. Facilitating communication and dialogue that provides all participants in the collaborative process with new insights into one another's culture, thereby empowering all individuals (Leake & Black, 2005)

Leake and Black (2005) presented a four-step process for the effective use of cultural reciprocity. Step 1 is for special education personnel to ask themselves why something they wish to suggest to a CLD family might be important for the family to consider (e.g., Why is it important to recommend to the family that their child with a developmental disability eventually live independently outside of the family home?). This allows for the special education personnel to engage in self-reflection and to explore their own cultural values (e.g., independence and self-sufficiency are widely held American values and recommended postsecondary outcomes of IDEA of 2004 [PL 108-446]). Step 2 is to compare these values and assumptions with those of the youth with the disability and his or her family (e.g., a CLD family might feel that it is the family's lifelong responsibility to care for the child with a disability in their home). Step 3 involves acknowledging cultural differences and maintaining an open and respectful discussion with the youth and family so that all individuals can gain an understanding of one another's perspectives (e.g., the transition personnel shares with the CLD family how independent living has benefited other youth with disabilities and their families; the family reiterates the overarching cultural value of family responsibility). Step 4 involves exploring the most effective way(s) in which special education personnel can adapt their professional interpretations and recommendations to the family's value system (e.g., the transition personnel either help the CLD family understand that there may come a time when they can no longer provide the care needed by their child or simply accept that this is not an appropriate postsecondary goal for this family and youth).

Despite its advantages, there are two barriers to the use of cultural reciprocity: 1) Extensive time may be needed to get to know a CLD youth with a disability and his or her family well enough in order to engage in this type of dialogue, and 2) it is a mistake to assume that special education personnel must be of a CLD heritage to work effectively with a CLD youth with a disability and his or her family (Kalyanpur & Harry, 1999). Kalyanpur and Harry (1999) cautioned that a culturally reciprocal approach to collaboration with CLD families of youth with disabilities should not be seen as a bag of tricks to be used to avoid conflict in emergency situations; rather, it should be embraced by special education professionals as an internalized value that is applicable in all interactions with CLD families (e.g., notes sent home, phone conferences, face-to-face meetings). With respect to the second barrier, research has shown that special education personnel can create effective partnerships with CLD families with whom they have little or no cultural affiliation. The issue is not one of shared culture, ethnic background, race, SES, or gender. Rather, the key to effective cultural reciprocity is the willingness of special education personnel to 1) seek to understand and learn about another individual's experiences, 2) ex-

IMPLICATIONS FOR PRACTICE

The first step in engaging in cultural reciprocity is to ask yourself why something you suggest to a CLD family might be important for them to consider. You should be mindful of the cultural norms and preferences of each family.

Engaging in cultural reciprocity involves acknowledging cultural differences and maintaining an open and respectful discussion with the youth and family so that all individuals can gain an understanding of one another's perspectives.

Kalyanpur and Harry (1999) cautioned that a culturally reciprocal approach to collaboration with CLD families should not be seen as a bag of tricks to be used to avoid conflict in emergency situations.

plore how their own individual experiences have shaped them as individuals, and 3) respect and accept the differences between these two sets of experiences. The case study of George Polomalu illustrates the use of cultural reciprocity in special education.

George Polomalu's Transition IEP

George Polomalu is a 17-year-old native Hawaiian student with a learning disability. He is on track to graduate high school with a diploma but has struggled in school and is not motivated to pursue postsecondary education. He lives at home with his mother, father, and two sisters (one older and one younger). His parents both work in the hospitality/ tourist industry, and the whole family is involved in Polynesian cultural entertainment (music, dancing, and singing). His high school special education teacher, Ms. Brown, is a White woman in her early 20s who was trained in special education at a university in southern California. She left the mainland 2 years ago and moved to Hawaii to pursue her first job in special education at George's high school. She is conducting a transition planning meeting at which George and his mother are present.

The meeting begins with introductions and a review of George's current level of performance (i.e., standardized test scores), grades, and completed credits toward his high school diploma. They then discuss postsecondary goals for George's remaining years in high school and beyond. Ms. Brown asks George whether he has considered attending college after he graduates. George responds that he is not really interested in college and is "kind of burnt out on school." Ms. Brown responds, "You know George, when I was growing up, my parents used to tell me a quote by President John F. Kennedy: 'To get a good job, get a good education.'" George shrugs his shoulders in response. At this point Mrs. Polomalu speaks up and says, "You know, Ms. Brown, in our culture it is not always necessary to go to college to get good work in Hawaii. It certainly helps in the long run, but many of us start out in the hospitality business, or tourism, or entertainment and make a decent living." Ms. Brown responds, "I appreciate what you are saying, Mrs. Polomalu. Over time I've begun to see that things are different here than on the mainland. I can accept that. But what about George moving out of the house and living on his own? Isn't that important to you, George?" George responds, "Maybe someday. Maybe after I get married and have a family of my own." Mrs. Polomalu adds, "Hawaiian families don't do things that way, Ms. Brown. We live together, love together, and extend ourselves to one another. The whole community raises a child, not just the immediate family. George has spent as much time with his aunties and uncles in his life as he has spent at home. He will always have a place to live wherever he wants in this community." Ms. Brown responds, "So, George, independent living is not a high priority for you in the near future?" "No, ma'am," replies George. "All right then," says Ms. Brown, "I guess we won't include that as one of your postsecondary goals, as neither you nor your family seems concerned about this."

Ms. Brown asks George what he would like to do after he finishes high school. George is a very talented Polynesian entertainer who is an exceptional dancer, musician (he plays several musical instruments), and singer. He has been performing since he was a small child in the family Polynesian entertainment group. George responds to Ms.

Brown's question by saying, "I would like to continue performing more full time with my family's group for awhile and maybe someday consider starting my own group or going to music school to perfect my music." Ms. Brown responds, "Those sound like excellent goals for you, George, and ones that you are very likely to succeed in accomplishing. Let's map out a plan for the next several years that will help you move in this direction. But before we do this, let me ask your mom if she is okay with this or has anything to add." Mrs. Polomalu responds, "I think this is great. It would make all of us very proud if George were able to do these things. We've known since he was very little that he had extra special talents in music and dancing. These are things that he is motivated to do, and that's always been half the battle with George—getting him involved in things he loves and can do!" The meeting ends with the completion of George's transition IEP and the refinement of postsecondary goals that correspond to his desires and wishes and those of his family.

Many examples of culturally responsive collaboration, as recommended by Lynch and Hanson (2004) were present in the transition IEP meeting of George Polomalu. Ms. Brown 1) demonstrated an openness, appreciation, and respect for the Polynesian culture despite it being different from her own; 2) utilized the interaction with George and his mother as a learning opportunity; and 3) was willing to utilize cultural resources in planning George's IEP goals. In addition, Ms. Brown demonstrated an awareness of her own cultural limitations when she said, "Over time I've begun to see that things are different here than on the mainland."

WHAT ARE RECOMMENDED PRACTICES IN CULTURALLY RESPONSIVE TRANSITION PLANNING WITH CLD FAMILIES OF YOUTH WITH DISABILITIES, AND WHAT DO THESE LOOK LIKE IN PUBLIC SCHOOLS?

Despite the wealth of literature that exists on the more general topic of recommended practices in transition planning for youth with disabilities (see Kochhar-Bryant & Greene, 2009, Wehman & Wittig, 2009, and Valenzuela & Maring, 2005 for an extensive discussion), a paucity of literature exists on recommended practices in transition planning for CLD families and youth with disabilities. Greene (1996) was one of the first to address the transition needs of CLD families of youth with disabilities by discussing topics such as 1) dimensions of culture and cultural diversity, 2) building rapport with CLD families, 3) factors affecting the participation of CLD families in the transition process, and 4) barriers to active CLD parent participation and advocacy. More in-depth analysis and discussion on the topic was presented by Greene and Kochhar-Bryant (2003), Kim and Morningstar (2005), and Kochhar-Bryant and Greene (2009), who recommended the following practices:

1. Develop increased knowledge and sensitivity about the multiple dimensions of cultural groups in IEP team members.
2. Use family-centered approaches and collaboration techniques when interacting with members of CLD groups.
3. Use effective communication practices with members of CLD groups.
4. Promote increased knowledge of and comfort with school policy, practices, and procedures with CLD families.

A list of culturally responsive recommended practices in transition planning with CLD families and youth with disabilities based on these works and several others appears in Table 2.3. A review of each of these recommended practices and the literature from which they were derived follows.

Cultural Reciprocity/Effective Communication with CLD Families

It is essential that professionals demonstrate a posture of cultural reciprocity and skilled dialogue when engaged in transition planning with CLD families and youth with disabilities. Failure to do so can result in writing a transition IEP that is irrelevant or invalid for the youth and his or her family. I reviewed most of the essential components and skills related to cultural reciprocity and skilled dialogue with CLD families and youth with disabilities in the previous section. Although the literature reviewed was written in the context of special education services in the public schools (e.g., assessment, placement, IEP meetings), it applies equally as well to interactions with CLD families and youth with disabilities in the context of transition planning.

The use of effective communication is another recommended practice when interacting with CLD families and youth with disabilities in the transition process (Kochhar-Bryant

Table 2.3. Culturally responsive recommended practices in transition planning with culturally and linguistically diverse (CLD) families and youth with disabilities

Recommendation	Supportive literature
Cultural reciprocity/effective communication with CLD families	Barrera and Corso (2003) Greene and Kochhar-Bryant (2003) Harry (1992, 2008) Kochhar-Bryant and Greene (2009) Lai and Ishiyama (2004) Leake and Black (2005)
Person-centered planning/family-centered approaches	Kochhar-Bryant and Greene (2009) Leake and Black (2005) Trainor (2007)
Cultural competence training for special education and transition personnel	Barrera and Corso (2003) Brandon (2007) Harry (1992, 2008) Kochhar-Bryant and Greene (2009) Leake and Black (2005)
CLD parent training to promote active participation in special education and transition planning meetings	Kochhar-Bryant and Greene (2009) Lai and Ishiyama (2004) Trainor (2007)
Self-determination training for CLD youth with disabilities	Gil-Kashiwabara et al. (2007) Kochhar-Bryant and Greene (2009) Leake and Black (2005)
CLD parent support groups, mentors, and community liaisons	Brandon (2007) Harry (1992) Kochhar-Bryant and Greene (2009) Landmark et al. (2007) Trainor (2007)

& Greene, 2009). One helpful strategy is to use interpreters familiar with the culture of the family in transition planning meetings. Another is to involve professional interpreters who are trained in the basics of special education and transition law and who can translate this information into a form that is relatively easy for CLD families and youth with disabilities to understand (Lai & Ishiyama, 2004). Lai and Ishiyama stated that "having interpreters who verify with the speakers as to underlying beliefs or values, and translate nonverbal behavior, such as polite disagreement, is especially important when tensions are running high" (p. 106). The case study of Wen Lee offers an example of involving a trained interpreter (i.e., Ms. Wong) capable of communicating with the CLD family in the transition planning process. Kochhar-Bryant and Greene cautioned that it is inappropriate to use other children or members of the family as interpreters in transition meetings because they may not possess adequate English skills to understand the complexities of the transition process or the vocabulary. Moreover, the use of children as interpreters may place the children in an inappropriate position of power in the parents' eyes, which is a particular concern in cultures that are hierarchical in nature.

Another strategy for promoting effective communication with CLD families in transition meetings is being aware of the high-context communication that characterizes certain cultures (Kochhar-Bryant & Greene, 2009). For example, "extensive verbal directiveness may be perceived as mechanistic and insensitive by Asians, Native Americans, Hispanics, and African Americans" (p. 452). Lynch and Hanson (2004; see also Lynch & Hanson, 2011) recommended the following communication practices when interacting with CLD families in special education:

1. Speak more slowly.
2. Listen more.
3. Observe family communication patterns (i.e., who speaks for the family).
4. Be aware of nonverbal behaviors or gestures (i.e., eye contact, body language).
5. Consult cultural guides or mediators in the community regarding communication recommendations.

Culture can influence styles of communication in transition planning meetings (Leake & Black, 2005). For example, Hispanic and Asian families may have culturally established styles of interacting with others that are "characterized by roles based on hierarchy, deference to authority, indirect confrontation, and maintenance of harmony and good relations" (p. 29). Leake and Black cautioned that because teachers are often viewed as being in positions of authority, some CLD parents may be hesitant to ask questions for fear of being perceived as challenging a teacher's authority. Valenzuela and Martin (2005) provided suggestions to bridge the values of diverse cultures and student-directed IEPs.

Person-Centered Planning/Family-Centered Approaches

Person-centered transition planning, also referred to as *family-centered approaches* to transition, is one of the most highly recommended practices in the transition literature. Traditional transition planning meetings have been criticized for being too professionally driven, with a focus on legalities, eligibility requirements, and the fitting of families to available transition programs and services rather than collaborative dialogue and family needs (Kochhar-

Bryant & Greene, 2009; Singer & Powers, 1993). Newer models of transition such as person-centered and family-centered approaches place a greater emphasis on recognizing the unique strengths of each individual family and youth with a disability, the importance of creating an equal relationship between these individuals and professionals, and the capacity of families and youth with disabilities to speak for themselves in the transition planning process. Kochhar-Bryant and Greene noted that the use of family-centered approaches promotes a sense of mutual trust, open communication, shared responsibility, and quality collaboration between professionals and CLD family members. This facilitates "a relationship that promotes more risk taking behavior and mutual involvement" (2009, p. 451).

The use of family-centered approaches promotes a sense of mutual trust, open communication, shared responsibility, and quality collaboration between professionals and CLD family members (Kochhar-Bryant & Greene, 2009).

One of the key aspects of person-centered planning (PCP) or family-centered approaches is that professionals take the time and make an effort to get to know the background of the youth and family (Leake & Black, 2005). Greene (1996, p. 27) suggested that professionals ask a number of important questions to help determine some of the key values of a CLD youth with a disability and his or her family:

1. What languages are spoken in the home and by which family members?
2. What are the family's norms for personal and social development for the youth with a disability (e.g., what degree of independence is encouraged)?
3. What residential and work-related goals for the youth with a disability are held by the family?
4. What are the family's views on disabilities, and how does this affect their view on treatment for their child?
5. How is the family conceptualized—as a nuclear unit or as an extended family structure?
6. What are the family's decision-making practices? Are they hierarchical, where the elders hold the decision-making power, or are they oriented toward individual rights with children expected to self-advocate?
7. How much legal knowledge about parents' rights and advocacy does the family possess?

These questions along with other important ones discussed earlier in the chapter are contained in the chapter appendix.

Trainor (2007) studied person-centered transition planning in two cultural communities (i.e., a Spanish-speaking community in a socioeconomically depressed urban area and an English-speaking community from a middle- and upper middle-class socioeconomic background). Several of the practices recommended here were included in this study. The individuals who conducted person-centered transition planning with the participants were 1) members of the families' communities and familiar with the backgrounds and cultures of the participants, 2) knowledgeable about the availability of and access to local transition resources, and 3) familiar with legal requirements related to transition and with special education policy and practice. The person-centered transition planning meetings in the study took place over the course of a year and attempted to connect youth with disabilities to community resources. Meetings took place in culturally appropriate settings for Latino families (e.g., over a cup of coffee or over a dinner in the family's home), and an equal, if not greater, amount of time spent with the parents or other members of the family was spent between the community connecters and the youth with disabilities. The results of the study demonstrated the efficacy of PCP as a tool for increasing family participation and self-determination and addressing the transition preferences, strengths, and needs of youth with disabilities. Moreover, the study demonstrated "the capacity for person-centered-planning methods to be implemented in a culturally responsive way" (Trainor, 2007, p. 99).

Research has demonstrated the efficacy of PCP as a tool for increasing family participation and self-determination and addressing the transition preferences, strengths, and needs of youth with disabilities (Trainor, 2007).

Two highly recommended PCP tools for transition are 1) the "circle of friends" and 2) the McGill Action Planning System (MAPS; Vandercook & York, 1989; see also Making Action Plans [MAPS]; Falvey et al., 1997). The circle of friends is a transition planning tool that provides a social scan of the youth with a disability to help identify the important people and activities in his or her life (Leake & Black, 2005). Based on the work of Falvey, Forest, Pearpoint, and Rosenburg (1997), the circle of friends method creates a visual representation of the youth's network of social support (see Figure 2.1). Four concentric circles are drawn that include the names of people who are increasingly more intimately involved with and close to the youth. According to Leake and Black, determining the important people in a youth's life allows the transition planning team to identify the most natural supports for the youth in as many situations as possible (e.g., community access, recreation, employment).

Another effective PCP tool for transition is MAPS. Kochhar-Bryant and Greene (2009) presented an example of MAPS, which they referred to as *Mapping*. Twelve questions are

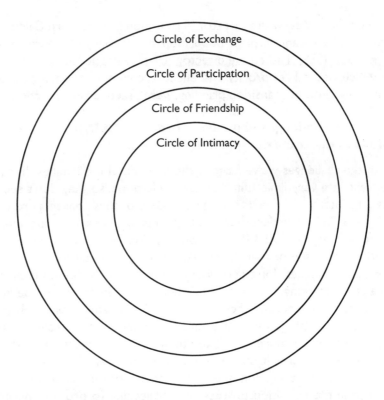

Figure 2.1. Circle of friends. (From Falvey, M.A., Forest, M., Pearpoint, J., & Rosenburg, R.L. [1997]. *All my life's a circle. Using the tools: Circles, MAPS & PATHS.* Toronto, Ontario, Canada: Inclusion Press; reprinted by permission.)

presented to the youth with a disability to help get to know him or her more closely and to assist the transition planning team in proposing transition goals. Examples of some of the Mapping questions follow (see the chapter appendix for the complete list of Mapping questions):

1. Who are the people in your life who interact with you on a regular basis?
2. Where do you typically spend your time?
3. What are things about you that people see as positive and make you likeable?
4. What are things about you that people see as negative and make you unlikeable?
5. What types of choices do you make?

PCP is just one of many transition assessment and planning methods (for a complete review of transition assessment, see Chapter 7 in Kochhar-Bryant & Greene, 2009). However, this particular transition planning method is particularly appropriate for use with CLD families and youth with disabilities, incorporates many of the principles of cultural reciprocity, and has been validated by research. For this reason, it is considered a recommended practice in transition planning with CLD families and youth with disabilities.

Interview with a Director of Transition Services in a School District with a Significant Hipanic Population

I conducted an interview with a director of transition in a southern California school district that has a significant Hispanic population, the majority of whom are of low socioeconomic status (SES). I asked the director several key questions to determine the degree to which cultural reciprocity and effective communication with CLD families, as well as person-centered transition planning, were practiced in the school district.

What are the challenges you have faced with CLD families and youth with disabilities in the transition planning process?

One of the challenges we've faced is the low SES of the families. In some instances the parents are very limited in their own education, so they don't see low academics as a barrier to their child's progress. Some of these parents are unable to read and have a limited understanding of the complexities of transition. Some don't understand that their child [has a disability], don't know what an IEP or the special education process is, or that their child was in special education.

Hispanic families don't necessarily want to openly discuss their child's disability in a public meeting or forum. The fathers or mothers may not be involved; either one may take the lead, and they see it's more of a family responsibility that should be handled in the home versus in public (i.e., home-based transition; family as value). The parents may be reticent to listen to and make connections with outside agencies because this "takes it outside the family"; there are language barriers; and they lack sophistication, education, and understanding of the details of the disability and their role in the transition process. It's challenging to provide these families with access to services that are disability related. Having a significant disability can be taboo in their culture.

What things have you tried and implemented to improve the quality of collaboration with CLD families of youth with disabilities in the transition planning process? What has been successful and what has not?

Speaking Spanish—coordinating the meeting in Spanish, discussing and presenting rights in Spanish. But how much the families understand is not always certain. A sophisticated level of Spanish communication is required. It takes time.

We have conducted presentations and parent seminars on careers in Spanish to increase the economic potential and opportunities for the CLD youth with disabilities. We have also talked about college and college acceptance with these families.

What would you recommend as best practices for collaboration with CLD families of youth with disabilities in the transition planning process?

I would recommend extra explanations to CLD families from the moment of special education identification. Provide them with ongoing, comprehensive overviews and information at an early age in Spanish, both orally and in writing, and check for understanding. Let them know about various agencies such as a state regional center, department of rehabilitation, and Department of Mental Health. Home-based meetings should take place with the families to cement the relationship, or find another comfortable setting in which to meet in case meeting in their home is not offered. Make sure you provide adequate time for the discussion. Provide technology that can be loaned to the home (e.g., DVD players, computers), or let them know of information distributed in venues outside of the school: local churches or faith centers, for example. Find a key community liaison and help them become knowledgeable.

We have been successful in many ways. Part of that success is because we speak Spanish and are willing to call a Spanish-speaking person to the meeting who is familiar with special education. Helping Spanish-speaking families make the initial connection with agencies that have Spanish-speaking representatives results in a smooth collaboration process.

Cultural Competence Training for Special Education and Transition Personnel

A study by Povenmire-Kirk et al. (2010) confirmed the need for professional development for people working with CLD families and marginalized youth with disabilities. However, they noted that in the school district they studied, cultural competence training was only one choice from among many professional development options offered rather than a requirement. This can potentially result in cultural competence training being taken by those who need it the least, a situation "that is much like preaching to the choir" (p. 49). In contrast, Harry stated that "both in-service and preservice preparation must be revised to place cross cultural education at the highest priority" (2008, p. 382). She made a number of specific recommendations regarding the content of preservice and in-service training for special educators collaborating with CLD families:

1. Coursework in multicultural histories and issues
2. Clarification of personal values regarding diversity
3. Critical perspectives on the assumptions and processes by which CLD children are placed in special education

4. Preparation and practice in actual cross-cultural communication

5. Internships and practicum placements in diverse racial and socioeconomic settings

Kim and Morningstar (2009) and Kochhar-Bryant and Greene (2009) discussed significant transition-related barriers for CLD youth with disabilities and their families. They organized these barriers into three categories: 1) professional insensitivity to cultural groups, 2) school-imposed barriers to transition, and 3) inherent characteristics of CLD groups. Informing special educators and transition personnel of these barriers and how to overcome them with CLD families is an important aspect of cultural competence training.

With respect to the first category, professional insensitivity to cultural groups, Kochhar-Bryant and Greene (2009) recommended that cultural competence training for professionals include information on

1. The dimensions of culture and cultural diversity (e.g., explorations of the meaning and characteristics of culture and cultural diversity, cultural models, beliefs, and practices)

2. Theories about cultural differences (e.g., ethnocentrism, assimilation, cultural model perspective)

3. The differences in values between the United States and other cultures (e.g., with regard to attitudes toward disabilities, individualism versus collectivism, family extendedness and interdependence, cooperative behavior, a holistic orientation to life)

Cultural competence training in the second category, school-imposed barriers to transition, should focus on reducing professional behaviors that act as deterrents to CLD parent participation in the transition planning process. Harry, Allen, and McLaughlin (1995) found five school-imposed barriers to African American parents' participation and advocacy for their children in special education conferences:

1. Late notices and inflexible scheduling of conferences (e.g., lack of advanced or too short notice to parents prior to a scheduled meeting, scheduling meetings for times when it was impossible for parents to attend)

2. Limited time for conferences (e.g., 20- to 30-minute conferences because of the need for teachers to return to classes, conferences scheduled before the start of school)

3. Emphasis on documents rather than participation (e.g., documents being mailed to parents to sign and parents being advised that they need not attend the meeting, parents perceiving their main role as one of a passive recipient of information)

4. The use of jargon (e.g., parents confused by unexplained jargon and technical terms contained in reports, resulting in them feeling intimidated at the conference)

5. The structure of power (e.g., interpersonal dynamics at the meeting placing parents at a distinct disadvantage, conferences in which power and authority were completely given to professionals)

With respect to the last category, inherent characteristics of CLD groups, Kochhar-Bryant and Greene (2009) recommended the following topics be included in cultural competence training:

1. Low SES (e.g., the effect of SES on the attitudes, perceptions, and receptiveness of school personnel toward CLD parents; stereotypes and beliefs held by professionals about CLD parents of low SES)

2. Attitudes toward disability (e.g., cultural variance in family response to having a child with a disability, cultural variance in attribution of the causes of disability, cultural attitudes about special education services)

3. Interpersonal communication style and differences in native language (e.g., the fact that in cultures that rely on high-context communication, words mean less than nonverbal cues, gestures, and body language; a non–English-speaking family's inability to understand information presented at a conference)

4. Knowledge and comfort with the school infrastructure (e.g., CLD parent lack of education, CLD parent general lack of understanding of school practices and procedures, CLD parent immigration status)

An evaluation instrument that measures the quality of CLD transition knowledge and skill in special education and transition personnel can be found in the chapter appendix. It can be used as a pre- and posttest for cultural competence transition training or as an instrument to measure the existing knowledge and skill in a school district or transition services agency. Information from the instrument can subsequently be used to design future staff development on the topic of cultural competence in transition services with CLD families and youth with disabilities. A sample agenda for a multiday staff development seminar of this nature is shown in Figure 2.2.

Cultural competence training can help build connections between schools and CLD families. Brandon (2007) addressed the issue of African American parent isolation from schools and provided specific suggestions to school personnel for how to increase these parents' connection with the educational environment. Examples of some of these suggestions include the following:

1. Improve school–home communication by
    a. Educators reflecting on their beliefs of how parents should communicate with schools
    b. Evaluating whether these beliefs affect the relationship with parents
    c. Developing a parent handbook that addresses questions commonly asked by parents

2. Promote interaction among the school, educators, and parents by
    a. Soliciting from parents the problems they encounter around the issue of school participation
    b. Asking parents about their perceptions of the racial climate of the school

A book by Barrera and Corso (2003) titled *Skilled Dialogue: Strategies for Responding to Cultural Diversity in Early Childhood* is an excellent resource for cultural reciprocity competence training. It provides an extensive review of the challenges faced by CLD families when collaborating with schools, an overview and comprehensive presentation of the components and intricacies of skilled dialogue, and an excellent set of forms and materials for special educators to use when practicing skilled dialogue with any age level.

CLD Parent Training to Promote Active Participation in Special Education and Transition Planning Meetings

Research has consistently demonstrated that CLD parents of youth with disabilities lack an understanding of transition law, their own rights and responsibilities, and available services in the community. This is one of the primary reasons they do not actively participate in transition planning meetings. Kochhar-Bryant and Greene (2009) offered some specific suggestions for ways to promote improved CLD family knowledge of school policy, practices, and

---

Agenda
Cultural Competence Training for Effective Transition
Planning with CLD Families and Youth with Disabilities

1. Make introductions
2. Present overview of training objectives, activities, and purposes
3. CLD Transition Knowledge and Skill Evaluation Instrument
    a. Administer pretest and summarize results.
    b. Discuss implications for competency training.
4. Present information on challenges faced by CLD families and youth with disabilities in the transition planning process.
    a. Lack of understanding of our culture and culture as a liability
    b. Lack of respect for our children and us
    c. Lack of acknowledgment of our hopes and dreams for our child's future
    d. Lack of understanding of the legal requirements for transition
    e. Racial and cultural stereotypes and biases of school professionals
    f. Immigration issues, lack of language proficiency, differences in cultural attitudes and norms affecting parents' views of transition for CLD youth with disabilities
    g. Generational conflict related to transition to adult life.
    h. Three barriers to successful transition for CLD families and youth with disabilities (i.e., professional insensitivity to cultural groups, school-imposed barriers to transition, inherent characteristics of CLD groups)
5. Define and discuss cultural reciprocity/effective communication with CLD families and youth with disabilities.
    a. Essential elements of cultural reciprocity
    b. Essential elements of skilled dialogue
    c. Effective communication with CLD families and youth with disabilities
6. Present information on person-centered planning (PCP) in transition.
    a. Essential elements of PCP
    b. Examples of PCP in transition
7. Discuss strategies, resources, and materials to increase active involvement of CLD parents and youth with disabilities in transition planning.
    a. Development of CLD parent outreach programs
    b. Use of community liaisons and mentors
8. Present CLD Transition Knowledge and Skill Evaluation Instrument
    a. Administer posttest and summarize results.
    b. Discuss implications for competency training.
    c. Create action plans, next steps for personnel attending the training.

Suggested materials and handouts:

PowerPoint slides and copies of slides for participants (Create your own as needed.)

CLD Transition Knowledge and Skill Evaluation Instrument

Table 2.1: Essential characteristics of effective collaboration

Table 2.2: Roles for parents of CLD youth with disabilities in special education

Case studies from this chapter

Appendix: Culturally Responsive Questions to Ask CLD Families of Transition-Age Youth with Disabilities, Person-Centered Planning/Family-Centered Questions for Getting to Know a CLD Family and Youth with a Disability (Greene, 1996), Mapping Questions

Figure 2.2. Sample agenda for a multiday staff development seminar on cultural competence in transition services. (*Key:* CLD, culturally and linguistically diverse.)

procedures in special education and transition. For example, because some CLD parents come from backgrounds in which schooling is seen as a privilege rather than a right, transition personnel must educate these families about legal mandates related to transition, postsecondary options, transition service agencies, and parental advocacy organizations. One suggested means of accomplishing this is through the use of parent outreach programs (Kochhar-Bryant & Greene, 2009). For example, Inger (1992) suggested that CLD parent support programs do the following:

1. Make it as easy as possible for parents to participate by
    a. Offering bilingual presentations and materials
    b. Providing child care
    c. Not charging fees
    d. Providing interpreters
    e. Providing transportation
    f. Scheduling meetings at convenient times and locations
2. Establish personalized, face-to-face, individualized contacts with parents, such as by meeting them in their homes if necessary
3. Disseminate information and gain access to parents through traditional community supports such as churches and ethnic organizations as opposed to impersonal efforts such as letters and fliers

In addition, Liontos (1991) suggested that successful CLD parent support programs include

1. An emphasis on parent and family strengths
2. Demonstration by program presenters that parents' strengths are valued
3. The teaching to parents of new techniques, capabilities, and means of overcoming obstacles

A sample CLD parent support program agenda is shown in Figure 2.3.

Many of the recommendations of Liontos (1991) were present in a study by Trainor (2007), who utilized community connecters to provide indirect training in PCP to CLD parents and youth with disabilities. Louise, one of the community connecters in the study and an English-speaking parent of a child with a disability, was a member of the social network of middle- to upper middle-class families with youth with disabilities that participated in the study. She was able to use this social network to help publicize the project to members of the community. In addition, she posted fliers and spoke directly to youth with disabilities to promote parent interest in the project. Elsie, a Latino community connecter, used a number of different, more culturally appropriate approaches with Latino families. She took

---

Agenda
1. Introductions
2. Statement of meeting purpose
3. Parent sharing: Tell us about your family (i.e., people in your home, children's ages and grades in school, one or two things about your family that are special to you).
4. Challenges and difficulties your family has faced at home, school, or in the community
5. Parents helping parents: Sharing ideas of things that have helped or worked for you to cope with or overcome challenges and difficulties
6. Some new ideas: Teach parents some new techniques.

Materials and handouts
Appendix: Culturally Responsive Questions to Ask CLD Families of Transition-Age Youth with Disabilities

---

Figure 2.3. Sample parent support program agenda. (*Key:* CLD, culturally and linguistically diverse.)

time to get to know the CLD youth with disabilities and their parents through activities in the classroom and community. She approached the parents and offered them PCP transition training only after she felt that enough trust had been established. She was quoted as saying, "And the families that I work with, there's something about our Latino culture; they'd say, 'Sure, come over and we'll have coffee,' and make it this dinner-type of thing" (Trainor, 2007, p. 96). Once the CLD parents were adequately trained in and comfortable with the PCP transition process, very positive outcomes occurred. For example, both trainers reported having a wide variety of participants attend PCP meetings for youth with disabilities. In addition to people mandated by special education law (e.g., general and special education teachers, transition specialists), family members, members of the youths' religious communities, adult friends of the youth and the family, coaches and extracurricular club sponsors, and related service providers attended the meetings. Note that it was the youth with disabilities and their parents who were responsible for inviting these members to attend the transition planning meetings. Something else worth noting about the PCP training provided to the CLD parents and youth with disabilities is the location where many of the meetings took place. Elsie, the Latino community connector, reported that the meetings occurred in the homes of the CLD youth with a disability. She said the following:

> So I try to keep it as informal as I can, and if they want to turn it into a dinner or a luncheon or whatever. Sometimes parents are very grateful for something you did in the beginning of the year, and they just take the opportunity to thank you. But that has not happened most of the time. (Trainor, 2007, p. 97)

Lai and Ishiyama (2004) also discussed the advantage of informal relationships for providing training to CLD parents of youth with disabilities. Several of the Chinese-Canadian mothers of youth with disabilities in their study preferred informal contact with the teacher as a means of understanding each other. For example, one parent in the study enjoyed a meeting "where the teachers conversed with the parents in a friendly manner and refreshments were served, 'like a tea party'" (p. 193). A list of 10 suggestions for informally establishing relationships appears in Table 2.4.

Finally, Trainor (2007) summarizes the value of providing CLD parents with quality training. Such training elevates the status of CLD family members and the youth with disabilities, thereby increasing their participation in the transition planning process.

Table 2.4. Ten suggestions for informally getting to know a culturally and linguistically diverse family and youth with disabilities

1. Have coffee or tea in the family's home or at a comfortable meeting place in the community.
2. Attend an extracurricular activity of the youth with a disability.
3. Enjoy a meal with them at their home or someplace in the community.
4. Go on an outing with them.
5. Attend religious services with them.
6. Meet them in a local park and spend time together.
7. Ask for permission to attend a family function.
8. Make a meal or dessert for them and share it together in a mutually comfortable location.
9. Take photographs of the youth with a disability and give them to the family.
10. Send a card for a special occasion (e.g., birthday, holiday, graduation).

Self-Determination Training for CLD Youth with Disabilities

Gil-Kashiwabara et al. (2007) noted the importance of educating marginalized youth with disabilities about what their opportunities and rights are, how to effectively ask for what they need, and how to work proactively with transition service providers in order to achieve their postsecondary goals. These collective skills and other related ones are referred to in the transition literature as *self-determination* and *self-advocacy*. Over the past several decades, transition leaders have strongly endorsed empowering all youth with disabilities to develop and demonstrate self-determination and self-advocacy. The Division on Career Development and Transition (DCDT) of the Council for Exceptional Children issued a position statement about the need to train youth with disabilities in self-determination and self-advocacy to facilitate their transition to adult life (Field, Martin, Miller, Ward, & Wehmeyer, 1988).

A variety of self-determination skills programs have been developed over the years. The most common elements of quality self-determination skills models and curricula for youth with disabilities are

1. Knowing yourself (e.g., your strengths, weaknesses, needs, preferences, dreams, priorities)
2. Accepting and valuing yourself
3. Developing goals and action plans
4. Acting on plans
5. Using feedback to evaluate outcomes and revising action plans as necessary

A list of published self-determination programs can be found in Table 2.5.

Teachers play an important role in the self-determination training of youth with disabilities. The development of self-determination skills is a long-term process that requires teachers to provide extensive practice to youth with disabilities in a variety of authentic roles and settings in which self-determination skills are needed. Skills should not be taught in iso-

Table 2.5.   Self-determination curricula for promoting transition skills in CLD youth with disabilities

Curricula	Authors	Features
The Choicemaker Self-Determination Transition Curriculum	Martin and Marshall (1994)	Targeted to help students acquire knowledge and skills that will give them a stronger voice in the IEP process
Next S.T.E.P.	Halpern et al. (1997)	Designed to teach students transition planning skills and the steps they need to successfully engage in the transition process
Steps to Self-Determination	Field and Hoffman (1996)	Contains strategies and materials that promote knowledge, skills, and values that lead to self-determination
TAKE CHARGE for the Future	Powers, Ellison, Matuszewski, Wilson, and Turner (1997)	Contains four major components or strategies designed to develop self-determination skills in youth both with and without disabilities
I-Plan	Van-Reusen and Boss (1990)	Designed to promote increased student involvement in educational planning and, in some cases, student-directed IEPs
Whose Future Is It Anyway?	Wehmeyer and Kelchner, (1995)	Contains 36 sessions that introduce the concept of transition and transition planning using student-directed materials and instructions

Key: CLD, culturally and linguistically diverse; IEP, individualized education program.

lation (e.g., in the classroom only) but in the context in which they will be used (e.g., in the school, home, or community).

Field, Martin, Miller, Ward, and Wehmeyer (1998, as cited in Kochhar-Bryant, Bassett, & Webb, 2009) offered a list of attributes that are typically associated with self-determined behaviors: awareness of personal preferences, interests, and needs; the ability to set goals; the ability to self-advocate; the ability to be persistent; the ability to be self-confident; and the ability to evaluate decisions.

Student-directed IEPs are another behavior associated with self-determination. Kochhar-Bryant and Greene (2009, p. 320) presented specific objectives for teaching youth with disabilities throughout their school years to promote their active involvement in IEP and transition planning meetings:

- Learn about your disability.
- Learn about IEP laws.
- Learn how to choose goals across transition areas.
- Learn how to participate in and lead your own IEP meeting.

In addition, they described what students can do before, during, and after IEP and transition planning meetings take place. Examples of things youth with disabilities can do *before the IEP meeting* include

1. Understanding what is supposed to happen during the meeting and asking a teacher to explain if they are unsure
2. Brainstorming about who to invite to the meeting and inviting these individuals to attend
3. Reviewing their dreams and goals for the future
4. Writing out any questions they may have
5. Learning to lead the meeting

Examples of things youth with disabilities can do *during the meeting* include

1. Speaking clearly about their thoughts, feelings, and dreams for the future
2. Being open to the suggestions and ideas of others and to transition activities that can help them reach their goals
3. Asking questions about things they do not understand

Examples of things youth with disabilities can do *after the meeting* include

1. Continuing to talk and check in regularly with other supportive adults and transition personnel about their transition plan
2. Following through on what they agreed to do and asking for help if needed
3. Making sure that the activities agreed upon in their plan take place
4. Modifying their plan as they mature or their interests change

More suggestions of activities for developing self-determination are included in Table 2.6.

Although a wealth of literature, materials, and programs have been developed to provide training in self-determination and self-advocacy skills to youth with disabilities, Leake and Black stated that "virtually all available self-determination programs and curricula are

Table 2.6. Ten things youth with disabilities can do to develop self-determination skills

1. Make a list of your preferences and interests.
2. Draw pictures of things that you consider to be your strengths.
3. Write down ways that you learn best.
4. Tell somebody your hopes and dreams for the future.
5. Explore available options to help you achieve your goals.
6. Make a plan of the steps to achieve your goals in the next 6 months, 1 year, 3 years, and 5 years.
7. Identify people and resources that can help you achieve your goals and implement your plan.
8. Identify things that will indicate whether your plan is working.
9. Discuss what you can do if things do not go according to your plan.
10. Rehearse and practice various aspects of your plan.

based on American mainstream values that may be at odds with the values of CLD cultures" (2005, p. 10). Therefore, many of these programs may need to be adapted in order to be relevant and effective for CLD youth with disabilities. For example, mainstream American culture is individualistic, whereas other cultures are more collectivist. Personnel engaged in culturally sensitive self-determination and self-advocacy training would teach CLD youths with disabilities how to advocate and make choices for themselves within the context of defined roles and expectations within their culture versus making choices that are independent of their family and cultural community. Effective self-advocacy requires that an individual develop assertiveness and problem-solving skills; being assertive in some cultures is considered negative, especially when young people are considered low in the social hierarchy (Leake & Black, 2005). Other aspects of self-advocacy that might be at odds with particular cultural values includes a CLD youth with a disability disclosing to others the personal challenges that he or she is facing or asking strangers for help. These aspects of self-determination and self-advocacy may increase conflict and lead to confrontation with the family. "Self-advocacy training therefore needs to include a focus on how to appropriately interact in different settings" (p. 12).

Many self-determination programs and curricula are based on mainstream American values and may need to be adapted in order to be relevant and effective for CLD youth with disabilities (Leake & Black, 2005).

Leake and Black (2005) noted some culturally sensitive curricula for teaching self-advocacy and self-determination skills. These are available from the Self-Determination Synthesis Project, which identified about 50 data-based research interventions shown to be effective in teaching specific self-determination skills. One of the interventions in the project is unique because it was developed specifically for low-income CLD high school students. The materials include lesson plans, lesson objectives, setting and materials, lesson content, teaching procedures, and evaluation methods. These can be downloaded for free from http://www.uncc.edu/sdsp/sd_lesson_plans.asp

Despite these considerations, transition personnel should not stop promoting self-determination and self-advocacy in CLD youth with disabilities. Leake and Black (2005) contend that only a small number of CLD families are likely to react negatively to this training for their children. Therefore, transition personnel should strive to provide CLD youth with disabilities transition training in these essential skills in a culturally sensitive manner.

CLD Parent Support Groups, Mentors, and Community Liaisons

The use of parent support groups, mentors, and community liaisons is another way to facilitate better collaborative relationships among CLD families of youth with disabilities, special educators, and transition personnel. Harry (1992) was an early advocate of utilizing CLD community members in this way. She noted that traditional advocacy training strategies do not work well with minority families because only a fraction of CLD parents are "well-to-do and well educated enough" to engage in such practices (p. 110). Harry instead recommended educating minority community leaders in the central issues faced by CLD families of youth with disabilities. Indeed, Brandon (2007) made similar recommendations some 15 years later with respect to African American parents of youth with disabilities. He observed that schools often lack a structured system that connects parents to the school and promotes parent ownership. He suggested establishing school committees run by African American parents in order to offer the parents input into school policy and procedures as well as provide them with networks of support. Brandon recommended that the implementation of parent support groups for African Americans include the following elements:

1. Regular committee meetings with the school principal and other educators
2. The creation of parent questionnaires that focus on obtaining critical input from African American parents on a variety of issues relevant to them (e.g., work schedules, parent conferences, transportation, child care, the inclusion of diversity in all facets of the school environment)
3. The creation of parent and educator modules designed to increase communication between African American parents of youth with disabilities and educators

Parent support groups should offer CLD parents of youth with disabilities information on district special education policies, materials and processes, and parental rights (Harry, 1992). These groups can encourage CLD parent advocacy by demonstrating that school personnel are open to the parents' perspectives and willing to listen to their thoughts and wishes on special education issues. This was validated in my own research when I spoke to members of the Chinese Parents Association for the Disabled (CPAD) in San Gabriel, California. Comments from CPAD parents reflecting their need to advocate and to be listened to by school personnel included 1) "It needs to be a team effort; we need to know each other well and communicate on a regular basis," 2) "We need more information and connection with future services for our child," 3) "The goal is to get the kids out and integrated into society," 4) "Getting the parents together to talk is very helpful," and 5) "Knowing that you are not the only family of a child with a disability helps with acceptance." Similarly, Asian American parents in a study by Landmark et al. (2007) requested the opportunity to be involved in parent support groups so that they could learn from other parents and professionals. Taken collectively, these findings and comments reinforce the thoughts of Kochhar-Bryant and Greene, who stated that special education and transition personnel "*must* [italics added] provide CLD parents with access to all sorts of information about transition…postsecondary options and service agencies for their youth with disabilities, and parent advocacy organizations" (2009, p. 453).

A number of studies have validated the strength of CLD parent support groups and mentors. For example, Trueba and Delgado-Gaitan (1988) demonstrated the validity of using CLD community mentors as support providers. Hispanic students, regardless of social status, who had academic mentors from their community successfully completed school as opposed to dropping out. Trainor (2007) also demonstrated the value of utilizing a CLD community connecter to facilitate effective PCP transition planning with CLD parents and youth with disabilities. Key design components of her study were the similarity of the backgrounds of the community connecter and parents and the fact that the community connecter resided in the same community and was acquainted with the CLD families she served. Finally, Geenen et al. (2003) demonstrated the strength of CLD parent support groups. Findings from focus groups and individual interviews with families representing a variety of cultures validated the resources and strengths these CLD families can provide transition service providers. Geenen et al. stated the following:

> Perhaps the most important strength is the connection many minority families have with their extended family and community. Indeed, professionals may be missing a significant resource in assisting families if they fail to forge partnerships with significant community leaders and informal support providers. (2003, p. 44)

Parent Support Group Resources for CLD Families of Youth with Disabilities

The Technical Assistance ALLIANCE for Parent Centers (also known as the ALLIANCE) is an innovative partnership of one national and six regional parent technical assistance centers. Each center is funded by the U.S. Department of Education's Office of Special Education Programs and offers parents of youth with disabilities technical assistance and coordination with the more than 100 Parent Training and Information Centers (PTIs) and Community Parent Resource Centers (CPRCs) established under IDEA. A number of PTIs and CPRCs (including the CPAD in San Gabriel, California) are specifically designed to help CLD families of youth with disabilities. Contact the ALLIANCE for information on how find a PTI or CPRC in your region.

SUMMARY

Engaging in culturally responsive transition planning is a key component of forming quality collaborative relationships with CLD families and youth with disabilities during the transition years. The ability of special education and transition personnel to be competent in the use of cultural reciprocity, PCP, and skilled dialogue greatly facilitates a successful outcome. This chapter outlined a number of recommended practices for interacting with CLD families and youth with disabilities during the transition process. Most, if not all, of these practices have been validated by research. Special education and transition personnel must be properly trained in order to effectively implement them in practice. This chapter offers resources, materials, and training guidelines for accomplishing this important objective. Likewise, it discusses how to provide training and assistance to CLD parents and youth with disabilities to promote their active involvement in transition planning and implementation. This information, if acted on appropriately by special education and transition personnel, should result in stronger partnerships with CLD families and youth with disabilities and more culturally responsive transition planning in the future.

Culturally Responsive Questions to Ask CLD Families of Transition-Age Youth with Disabilities

1. Do you understand and read English, or would you like us to provide an interpreter at the meeting and written information in your home language?
2. How do your family and cultural community view the role of education in your child's life?
3. How do your family and cultural community feel about children with disabilities?
4. What resources are available within your family and in your cultural community that you might consider using to help your child with a disability?
5. All of us have thoughts and ideas about what is best for your child, but we would really like to hear your thoughts today. Would you be willing to share some of them with us?
6. Is there anything we should know about your family or cultural community that can help us provide the best education possible for your child?

Person-Centered Planning/Family-Centered Questions for Getting to Know a CLD Family and Youth with a Disability (Greene, 1996)

1. What languages are spoken in the home and by which family members?
2. What are the family's norms for the personal and social development of the youth with a disability (e.g., what degree of independence is encouraged)?
3. What residential and work-related goals for the youth with a disability are held by the family?
4. What are the family's views on disabilities, and how do these affect the family members' views of treatment for the child?
5. How is the family conceptualized—as a nuclear unit or as an extended family structure?
6. What are the family's decision-making practices? Are they hierarchical, such that the older adults hold the decision-making power, or are they oriented toward individual rights, with children expected to self-advocate?
7. How much legal knowledge about parents' rights and advocacy does the family possess?

(continued)

(continued)

Mapping Questions (Kochhar-Bryant & Greene, 2009)

1. Who are the people in your life who interact with you on a regular basis?
2. Where do you typically spend your time?
3. What are things about you that people see as positive and make you likeable?
4. What are things about you that people see as negative and make you unlikeable?
5. What types of choices do you make?
6. What type of things do you prefer, motivate you, and make you happy?
7. What things do you not prefer, frustrate you, and make you unhappy?
8. What are your personal goals and dreams?
9. What are your most important priorities in the next several months to a year and in the next 1 to 5 years?
10. What people or agencies can help you achieve these personal goals and dreams?
11. What, if any, are potential barriers that can interfere with you achieving your personal goals and dreams?
12. What strategies can be used to help you overcome these obstacles or barriers?

CLD Transition Knowledge and Skill Evaluation Instrument

The purpose of this survey is to determine the degree to which transition services personnel within your school or agency possess *knowledge* (i.e., awareness, information, understanding) and *skills* (i.e., ability to design, create, implement in practice) to effectively collaborate with culturally and linguistically diverse (CLD) families in the transition planning process for youth with disabilities. The survey assesses knowledge and skills independent of one another. This is because transition personnel conducting transition planning with diverse families may 1) have limited to inadequate knowledge and skills, 2) have adequate knowledge but inadequate skills, or 3) have adequate knowledge and skills in this regard. Hence, it is important that all parts of the survey be completed in order to form valid and reliable conclusions. Please refer to the rating scale descriptors below when completing the survey. Thank you for your participation.

1 = inadequate   2 = needs improvement   3 = good   4 = excellent

Circle the number that best describes the quality of *knowledge* and *skills* of transition personnel with respect to working with diverse families of youth with disabilities during the transition planning process.

Section I: General Characteristics of Cultural and Linguistic Diversity

Family values, beliefs, and practices: Some of the following characteristics, although not restricted to families identified as CLD, may be more common to these families.

- Desire to maintain connection to and identification with their primary culture
- Desire to continue to speak and communicate in their primary language
- Favoring of family interdependence and connectedness versus independent identity
- Variation in child-rearing practices and defined roles for mothers and fathers, brothers and sisters, older adults and extended family and friends in the home and community
- High value on staying connected to parents and taking care of parents as they age

1. Rate the degree to which transition personnel in your school, school district, or agency possess knowledge and skills about the CLD family values, beliefs, and practices represented in your service area.

Knowledge	1	2	3	4
Skills	1	2	3	4

(continued)

(continued)

Family integration and acculturation status: Within a given immigrant family (e.g., Koreans, Latinos, Chinese), values, beliefs, and practices may vary depending on the length of time in the United States, generational status (e.g., first, second, or third-generation), and degree of acculturation to U.S. society.

1. Rate the degree to which transition personnel in your school, school district, or agency possess knowledge and skills about these possible variations.

   Knowledge   I   2   3   4

   Skills   I   2   3   4

CLD family attitudes and beliefs related to disabilities: All families vary in their attitudes and beliefs about disabilities. For example, some may have open and accepting attitudes and beliefs about disabilities and want their child to be fully included in school and society. Some families may feel a sense of shame or embarrassment about disabilities and do not want their child to be fully included in school or society.

1. Rate the degree to which transition personnel in your school, school district, or agency possess knowledge and skills about family attitudes and beliefs related to disabilities typical in your service area.

   Knowledge   I   2   3   4

   Skills   I   2   3   4

CLD family interpersonal communication style: The typical interpersonal communication style in the United States is one of *low context* (e.g., heavy reliance on precise, direct, and logical communication; self-advocacy; speak one's mind). In contrast, members of other cultures and families of lower socioeconomic status (SES) or with lower levels of literacy may use more *high-context* interpersonal communication (e.g., reliance on nonverbal cues, gestures, body language, and facial expressions; deference to authority; nonconfrontational language). Though not specific to the presence of cultural and linguistic diversity, members of communities identified as CLD may also use a high-context style when there are concomitant low levels of SES or literacy.

1. Rate the degree to which transition personnel in your school, school district, or agency possess knowledge and skills about the impact of low SES and literacy levels on interpersonal communication style typical in your service area.

   Knowledge   I   2   3   4

   Skills   I   2   3   4

CLD family structure and norms: A CLD family's structure and norms may differ from those of special education personnel. Some cultures are more patriarchal (i.e., fathers

(continued)

(continued)

are the primary authority figures in the home), value family identity and interconnect-edness (versus individualism), and may have more clearly defined roles and expectations for males and females, mothers and fathers, and brothers and sisters in the family unit.

1. Rate the degree to which transition personnel in your school, school district, or agency possess knowledge and skills about CLD family structure and norms typical of your service area.

Knowledge	1	2	3	4
Skills	1	2	3	4

Section II: Quality of Transition Planning Meeting Practices

Promoting active involvement of CLD family members during meetings: Researchers have found that CLD families are more likely than members of the majority culture to be passive during transition planning meetings. In addition, certain cultural considerations and practices appear to be underutilized by school or transition agency personnel for increasing and encouraging more active involvement among CLD families. Several recommended practices for promoting the active involvement of CLD families in transition planning meetings are listed below.

1. Rate the degree to which transition personnel in your school, school district, or agency possess knowledge and skills about ways to promote more active CLD family involvement in transition planning meetings.

   a. Provide adequate advanced notice of meetings.

Knowledge	1	2	3	4
Skills	1	2	3	4

   b. Schedule meetings at a convenient time for families (e.g., evening hours after work, weekends).

Knowledge	1	2	3	4
Skills	1	2	3	4

   c. Schedule meetings at a convenient location for families (e.g., family home, community center, religious institution).

Knowledge	1	2	3	4
Skills	1	2	3	4

(continued)

(continued)

d. Provide child care if needed during the meetings.

Knowledge   I   2   3   4

Skills   I   2   3   4

e. Provide a bilingual, bicultural translator during the meeting who is familiar with special education law and parent legal rights and who can explain special education jargon and terminology in a way that the family understands.

Knowledge   I   2   3   4

Skills   I   2   3   4

f. School or transition agency personnel communicate with all CLD family members in a way that makes them feel that they are equal partners with equal decision-making power during the meeting (e.g., by utilizing person-centered transition planning).

Knowledge   I   2   3   4

Skills   I   2   3   4

Section III: Quality for Promoting CLD Family Knowledge of School or Transition Agency Policies, Practices, and Procedures

CLD family understanding of legal aspects of transition: Individuals with Disabilities Education Improvement Act (IDEA) of 2004 (PL 108-446) transition legal requirements can be confusing to CLD families who are not familiar with the law or fully proficient in English. Likewise, eligibility requirements for adult transition services and support agencies can be complex and confusing, particularly when forms need to be completed and submitted in order to be determined eligible to receive services. Several recommended practices for promoting CLD family knowledge of school or transition agency policies, practices, and procedures are listed below.

I. Rate the degree to which transition personnel in your school, school district, or agency possess knowledge and skills about ways to promote CLD family knowledge and understanding of transition policies, practices, and procedures.

a. Explain transition legal mandates in a way that CLD families adequately understand these laws.

Knowledge   I   2   3   4

Skills   I   2   3   4

(continued)

(continued)

b. Explain the eligibility requirements of postsecondary transition services and agencies in a way that CLD families adequately understand these requirements.

Knowledge | 2 3 4

Skills | 2 3 4

c. Provide access to CLD community members or CLD parents of youth with disabilities to act as mentors to assist CLD families involved in the transition planning process.

Knowledge | 2 3 4

Skills | 2 3 4

d. Meet with CLD families in nontraditional locations and in the community (e.g., churches, homes, ethnic organizations, community centers) to engage in face-to-face collaboration during the transition planning process.

Knowledge | 2 3 4

Skills | 2 3 4

Section IV: Additional Comments

In the space below, please write any additional comments or input related to the questions and feedback on this survey that you feel would be helpful. Thank you for completing this survey.

3

Transition Individualized Education Programs and Summary of Functional Performance Documents for Culturally and Linguistically Diverse Family Examples

Juan Carlos Martinez is a 16-year-old Mexican American 11th grader with a learning disability who attends a large high school in East Los Angeles. He comes from a Spanish-speaking family and has three younger siblings (one brother and two sisters). His parents both work in the local community; his father is a custodian for the city of Los Angeles, and his mother cleans houses for extra income. Juan Carlos takes general education classes and receives one period a day of Research Specialist Program (RSP) support for help with study skills, homework, reading, and writing. He functions academically around the sixth-grade level. He also receives ELL support from an ELL specialist who comes into the RSP classroom twice a week.

Cho Hee Dan is a 16-year-old Korean young woman with Down syndrome in 11th grade at a large high school in Koreatown of downtown Los Angeles. She comes from a Korean-speaking family and has two siblings (an older brother and a younger sister). Her father works at the Ford automobile corporation as the manager of quality control, and her mother is a stay-at-home mom. Cho Hee is enrolled in a special day class at her neighborhood high school. She has below-average cognitive skills, functions academically at the first-to second-grade level in most subjects, and has English oral language skills around a fifth-grade level. Korean is the primary language spoken at home, but her parents also are proficient in speaking English. Cho Hee's academic program has focused primarily on acquiring the basic academic and daily living skills needed to function at home and in the community.

Juan Carlos and Cho Hee share several things in common: They are both of transition age, and, according to IDEA 2004, they are both entitled to have a transition IEP that focuses on outcomes for their transition from school to postschool life. When they reach their 12th-grade year, their special education teachers are required to write a Summary of Functional Performance (SOP) document that summarizes a variety of information about Juan Carlos and Cho Hee that can be used by postsecondary transition support personnel and agencies to provide quality adult services. The purpose of this chapter is to provide key information about transition IEPs and SOPs for special education and transition personnel who work with CLD families and youth with disabilities. This chapter answers the following questions:

1. What is the rationale for writing transition IEPs and SOPs for youth with disabilities?
2. What are the legal requirements of IDEA 2004 with respect to transition IEPs and SOPs?
3. How can special education and transition personnel conduct transition assessments to obtain information needed for writing culturally responsive transition IEPs and SOPs?
4. What types of transition programs and services are available in high school and beyond that meet the needs of CLD families and youth with disabilities?
5. What are examples of quality, culturally responsive transition IEPs and SOPs?

This chapter presents information derived from special education law, the special education and CLD transition literature, case studies, and my own experience and recommendations to answer these questions. In addition, professionals can use transition assessment data from the case studies to craft sample culturally responsive transition IEPs and SOPs.

WHAT IS THE RATIONALE FOR WRITING TRANSITION IEPs AND SOPs FOR YOUTH WITH DISABILITIES?

Transition has historically been conceptualized in special education and vocational rehabilitation (VR) literature as movement from school to quality adult life for a youth with a disability. Transition IEPs and SOPs are legally mandated paperwork that contain critical information about a youth with a disability to facilitate his or her smooth transition from high school to postsecondary settings, supports, and quality adult life.

Transition IEPs and SOPs are legally mandated paperwork that contain critical information about a youth with a disability to facilitate his or her smooth transition from high school to postsecondary settings, supports, and quality adult life.

The primary rationale for transition IEPs and SOPs is rooted in special education law (i.e., IDEA 1990, 1997 [PL 105-17], 2004) and can be traced to the historically poor school and postschool outcomes of youth with disabilities. Since the passage of the Education for All Handicapped Children Act of 1975 (PL 94-142), which guaranteed free appropriate education (FAPE) for all individuals with disabilities in the United States, various studies have investigated the effectiveness of special education programs and services provided to youth with disabilities. The most comprehensive studies to date on this topic are the NLTS-1 and NLTS-2, which were reviewed in Chapter 1. These and other follow-up or follow-along studies have gathered long-term data on various special education quality indicators for youth with disabilities, such as high school graduation and dropout rates, participation in postsecondary education, employment, income, living arrangements, and leisure activities. Information from these studies is highly valid because the data compare individuals with and without disabilities on the same variables. Results have consistently demonstrated that compared with their peers without disabilities, individuals with disabilities fare less well on critical postschool outcomes despite having received special education services while in school, having had access to the general education curriculum, and having participated in state and local testing. Specifically, compared with their peers without disabilities, youth with disabilities are less likely to receive a standard high school diploma, drop out twice as often, enroll and complete postsecondary education programs at half the rate, and are employed at approximately one third the rate (32% compared with 81%; National Council on Disability, 2003; NLTS-2, 2005). Although the NLTS-2 has shown that some improvement has occurred, youth with disabilities continue to experience lower high school graduation rates, lower college entrance rates, and higher rates of poverty. Moreover, compared with their white peers with disabilities, CLD youth with disabilities fare even less well on key transition outcomes (Blackorby & Wagner, 1996; NLTS-2, 2005).

It is for these reasons that IDEA legislation in 1990, 1997, and 2004 established transition as a federal priority in special education law. Transition IEPs were written into IDEA legislation beginning in 1990 and continued to be a requirement in the reauthorization of IDEA in 2004. The SOP requirement was added to IDEA in 2004. The purpose of transition IEPs and SOPs is to assess strengths, interests, and preferences, and document specific measurable transition goals. They also designate specific transition support agencies and personnel to assist youth with disabilities in achieving a quality adult life after graduating from or completing high school. Writing quality transition IEPs and SOPs is a complex process involving multiple sources of information, personnel, and agencies. The complexities can be even greater when cultural and linguistic diversity is added to the equation. Before discussing the development of transition IEPs and SOPs, one should review IDEA 2004 transition requirements.

The purpose of transition IEPs and SOPs is to assess strengths, interests, and preferences, and document specific measurable transition goals. They also designate specific transition support agencies and personnel to assist youth with disabilities in achieving a quality adult life after graduating from or completing high school.

WHAT ARE THE LEGAL REQUIREMENTS OF IDEA 2004 WITH RESPECT TO TRANSITION IEPs AND SOPs?

Federal special education legislation historically focused on ensuring that children and youth with disabilities had access to FAPE. In the 1990s, IDEA expanded the scope of this educational preparation to include activities that would help prepare youth with disabilities for life after leaving school, such as attending college, receiving employment training, finding a job, living independently, and participating in the community. IDEA 2004 used the term *transition services* to refer to these various activities. According to Section 602 of IDEA 2004

> The term "transition services" means a coordinated set of activities for a child with a disability that is designed to be within a results-oriented process that is focused on improving the academic and functional achievement of the child with a disability to facilitate the child's movements from school to postschool activities, including postsecondary education, vocational education, integrated employment (including supported employment), continuing and adult education, adult services, independent living, or community participation. In addition, the law emphasized that transition services and activities must be based upon the individual student's strengths, taking into account the student's preferences and interests, and include instruction, related services, community experiences, the development of employment and other postschool adult living objectives, and, when appropriate, acquisition of daily living skills and functional vocational evaluation. (IDEA 2004, SEC. 602).

Kochhar-Bryant and Izzo (2006) noted that despite the early intervention transition documentation requirements for young children with disabilities, there was a lack of parallel requirements in special education law for youth with disabilities at the secondary level prior to the reauthorization of IDEA in 2004. They stated that the purpose of the SOP requirement is to provide essential information on youth with disabilities to postschool settings and transition service agencies, bridging the gap between high school and post–high school environments. It summarizes all relevant formal and informal assessment data in one document and uses it as a basis for recommendations regarding accommodations and services the student may benefit from in the future. In fact, an SOP is intended to meet the standards for indicating the presence of a disability in accordance with Section 504 of the Rehabilitation Act of 1973 (PL 93-112) and/or the

> *An SOP is intended to meet the standards for indicating the presence of a disability in accordance with Section 504 of the Rehabilitation Act of 1973 (PL 93-112) and/or the Americans with Disabilities Act of 1990 (PL 101-336; Kochhar-Bryant & Izzo, 2006).*

Americans with Disabilities Act of 1990 (PL 101-336; Kochhar-Bryant & Izzo, 2006), which make individuals with disabilities eligible for services and accommodations in adulthood. IDEA 2004 specified that a comprehensive SOP evaluation is not required before the termination of a youth's eligibility for special education due to graduation from secondary school with a standard diploma:

> For a child whose eligibility under special education terminates due to graduation with a regular diploma, or due to exceeding the age of eligibility, the local education agency shall provide the child with a summary of the child's academic achievement and functional performance, which shall include recommendations on how to assist the child in meeting the child's postsecondary goals. (IDEA 2004, § 614c[5])

In summary, the purpose and specific language of the IDEA 2004 transition requirements for transition IEPs and SOPs is to provide documentation on goals, activities, and critical information on youth with disabilities to promote their successful movement from school to postschool settings and receipt of services.

HOW CAN SPECIAL EDUCATION AND TRANSITION PERSONNEL CONDUCT TRANSITION ASSESSMENTS TO OBTAIN INFORMATION NEEDED FOR WRITING CULTURALLY RESPONSIVE TRANSITION IEPs AND SOPs?

Much has been written on the topic of transition assessment (see Greene, 2009, for a review). Miller, Lombard, and Corbey (2007) defined *transition assessment* to include a determination of the following information about a youth with a disability:

1. Abilities, attitudes, and interests
2. Work behaviors, levels of self-determination and self-advocacy
3. Interpersonal, academic, and independent living skills
4. Long-term, extended skills that can be used for planning purposes

Note that many of these topics directly correspond with IDEA transition services requirements that state that a transition IEP must be based on individual needs and must take into account the "strengths, preferences, and interests" (sec. 300,43[a][2]) of the youth with a disability.

Transition assessment helps a youth with a disability make informed choices about his or her future career development, vocational training, postsecondary education, community functioning, and personal and social skills (Greene, 2009). The Division on Career Development and Transition of the Council for Exceptional Children published a position paper that described transition assessment "as an umbrella term that includes career assessment, vocational assessment, and ecological or functional assessment practices" (Sitlington, Neubert, & Leconte, 1997, p. 70). Hence, transition assessment involves determining a variety of skills and abilities in a youth with a disability. For this reason, it should take place in a number of different environments that are as natural as possible to the youth with a disability and should involve a variety of individuals associated with these natural environments (e.g., the individual youth, his or her network of family and friends, school and transition personnel, community service providers). It is important that collaboration occur among these individuals so that they can determine the type of information needed and the most effective methods for gathering this information. It is also important that transition assessment be 1) student centered, 2) useful and understandable to all people involved, and 3) sensitive to cultural and ethnic diversity (i.e., capable of accurately reflecting the values, desires, and beliefs of CLD youth with disabilities and their families; Test, Aspel, & Everson, 2006).

> *Transition assessment helps a youth with a disability make informed choices about his or her future career development, vocational training, postsecondary education, community functioning, and personal and social skills (Greene, 2009).*

Special education and transition personnel conducting a transition assessment can use the culturally responsive assessment questions presented in the Chapter 2 appendix to start to get to know the CLD family and transition-age youth with a disability. Furthermore, they should incorporate into the assessment use of the principles and practices of culturally responsive transition planning and skilled dialogue discussed in Chapter 2. Additional questions modified from Greene (2009) that the CLD youth with a disability can answer in the presence of transition personnel conducting a transition assessment are the following:

1. What are my interests, aptitudes, and capabilities in school, at home with my family, at work, and in my community?

2. Where do I want to live, work, or go to school after completing high school, and how do these compare with the thoughts of my family?

3. What courses do I need to take in high school to graduate and prepare for my future, and what are the preferences of my family?

4. What are my strengths and areas where I need to improve my transition skills and how do these compare with the thoughts of my family?

5. What do I need to learn to be a fully functional member of my family and/or community? (p. 238)

IMPLICATIONS FOR PRACTICE

Transition assessment is a fluid process that can take place over multiple years. Ideas discussed in the process should be periodically revisited throughout the transition years of the youth with a disability to ensure that they are still appropriate.

In contrast to traditional assessment in special education, which is typically an annual process, transition assessment is an ongoing process that can take place over multiple years (Greene, 2009). Therefore, the answers to these questions can be considered fluid and should be periodically revisited throughout the transition years of the youth with a disability. Another key difference between transition assessment and traditional special education assessment is that the former is much more person centered and places an emphasis on the capabilities rather than the disabilities of the individual being assessed (Greene, 2009). For this reason, CLD families and youth with disabilities, as well as their non-CLD counterparts, may find the transition assessment process to be a positive and supportive experience (e.g., for CLD families, potentially devoid of culture as a liability, stereotypes, and the racial biases discussed in Chapter 1).

A case study of a transition assessment of Juan Carlos Martinez, the first of the two youths identified in the chapter opening, follows.

Juan Carlos Martinez's Transition Assessment

Mr. Jimenez is a Spanish-speaking high school special education teacher who is the case manager for Juan Carlos Martinez. Mr. Jimenez is an RSP teacher and has been seeing Juan Carlos for one period a day in the resource room since Juan Carlos began high school 2 years ago. This year, Juan Carlos has reached the age of 16 and therefore is entitled to a written transition IEP. Mr. Jimenez is conducting a transition assessment with Juan Carlos in preparation for writing the transition IEP. Mr. Jimenez has asked a variety of people, including Juan Carlos, for transition-related information and has conducted this assessment over the course of the past several months in a variety of settings (e.g., school, home, community).

Mr. Jimenez began the transition assessment by visiting Juan Carlos in his family's home one evening after school. Spanish was spoken the entire time, and after sharing coffee and dessert with the family, Mr. Jimenez began by asking Juan what he likes to do and what he is good at doing in school, at home, and out in the community. Juan Carlos said that school is hard for him, but because he knows how important it is to his family that he graduate with a diploma, he always tries his best. Mr. Jimenez agreed with Juan Carlos and assured his family that he would continue to provide the necessary support to help Juan Carlos pass the high school exit exam and graduate with a diploma. He asked Juan Carlos's parents whether this was an important transition goal that they would like to have included in the transition IEP for Juan Carlos; they overwhelmingly agreed.

"I know that school is a struggle for you, Juan Carlos. What things other than school give you pleasure and are things that you love to do and consider yourself good at doing?" asked Mr. Jimenez. Juan Carlos replied that he loves drawing and said, "I think I'm pretty good at it." Mr. Jimenez said that he has seen some of Juan Carlos's work and agreed that he has a real talent for art. He then asked Juan Carlos whether this is something he would like to do for work someday or possibly study further in the future to develop his talents. Juan Carlos smiled and said, "Most definitely!" Mr. Jimenez asked Juan Carlos's parents what they thought of this idea, and they expressed concern about whether their son could earn a living drawing. Mr. Jimenez responded, "I don't know and can't say, but I think it's worth exploring. Juan Carlos will graduate with a diploma and can go on to study art at a community college or 4-year university, possibly with a scholarship or financial aid, if he really has the talent and capability. I believe he does. However, in the meantime, would it be all right with you, Mr. and Mrs. Martinez, for me to write a transition goal in Juan Carlos's transition IEP to enroll him in a series of art classes at the high school or in a vocational training program in the community to further his skills? In addition, I would suggest we look into some job development for Juan Carlos at an art store to get him working in something he loves to do. What do you think?" Juan Carlos's parents nodded their heads in agreement. "How about you, Juan Carlos? What do you think about these transition goals?" Mr. Jimenez asked. Juan Carlos replied that he thought these would be great.

Mr. Jimenez then turned the discussion to the supports and resources Juan Carlos would need in the next several years in high school and afterward to successfully achieve his desired outcomes. These included continuing to work every day in the RSP classroom, working with the transition employment specialist to learn prevocational skills (i.e., skills related to searching for a job, completing a job application, interviewing, and retaining employment), and enrolling in art classes at the high school or community vocational training center. Mr. Jimenez cautioned Juan Carlos that he needed to keep his grades up; continue to meet his home and family responsibilities (i.e., help his mother care for his younger siblings); and maintain good behavior in school, at home, and in the community. His parents nodded their heads in agreement and support of these statements and said that if Juan Carlos were able to do these things, they would support his art-related activities.

The meeting ended with Mr. Jimenez telling the Martinez family that this information would be written into the transition IEP for Juan Carlos and presented to them for discussion and approval at an upcoming transition IEP meeting. They discussed possible dates and times and convenient locations for the meeting. Mr. Jimenez said that he would be sending to their home a formal letter written in Spanish confirming all that they had discussed this evening. Mr. Jimenez thanked the family for their time, and they expressed warmth to him as they saw him out.

The case study of Juan Carlos Martinez contains many of the CLD transition assessment practices discussed earlier in this chapter as well as some of the culturally responsive transition planning practices recommended in Chapter 2. For example, the meeting occurred at the family's home at a convenient time, was informal, and was conducted in Spanish. Although the transition assessment initially focused on Juan Carlos's thoughts, Mr. Jimenez demonstrated respect for the family by carefully following up with them to be sure that they supported the desires their son expressed. When Mr. and Mrs. Martinez shared their concerns about Juan Carlos being able to earn a living from art, Mr. Jimenez identified transition services and supports to Juan Carlos to maximize his capabilities and interests (i.e., art classes in high school, classes at the local vocational training school, job development, transition to a community college or 4-year university to continue studying art with financial aid or a possible scholarship). Finally, Mr. Jimenez showed respect for the family by emphasizing the importance of Juan Carlos attending to home responsibilities and providing support to his mother in caring for his younger siblings. Mr. Jimenez also emphasized the importance of Juan Carlos keeping up his grades and progress in school toward passing the high school exit exam, earning credits toward his diploma, and graduating, all of which were transition priorities for his parents.

Greene (2009) discussed how special educators can conduct transition assessment plans that provide relevant information to a CLD family and youth with a disability as well as other transition service providers. Sitlington et al. (1997) is a good resource for anyone just starting to develop a transition assessment plan. These authors proposed asking the following key questions to help guide the transition assessment process:

1. What do I already know about this individual that would be helpful in developing postsecondary outcomes?

2. What information do I need to know about this individual to determine postsecondary goals?

3. What methods will provide this information?

4. How will the assessment data be collected and used in the IEP process?

Figure 3.1 shows various knowledge and skill domains to consider when gathering transition assessment data on a youth with a disability (Sitlington & Clark, 2006). Figure 3.2 contains a transition assessment planning form developed by Greene (2009) from the questions of Sitlington et al. (1997). Special education personnel can use this form to write notes about a youth with a disability during the transition assessment process.

One transition assessment model that deserves mention is person-centered transition assessment and planning. This method was reviewed in Chapter 2. Person-centered transition assessment and planning, which includes methods such as Mapping and the circle of friends, is highly effective for use with CLD families and youth with disabilities because it is based on the input of these individuals. The method offers the opportunity for culturally responsive collaboration to occur among all parties involved in the transition assessment process (Greene, 2009).

Person-centered transition assessment and planning methods such as Mapping and the circle of friends are highly effective for use with CLD families and youth with disabilities because they are based on the input of these individuals.

The Making the Match transition assessment model (Sitlington, Neubert, Begun, Lombard, & Leconte, 1996) is another method that offers the opportunity to engage in culturally responsive transition assessment. This model is shown in Figure 3.3. This transition assessment method analyzes various aspects of the youth with a disability (e.g., cognitive

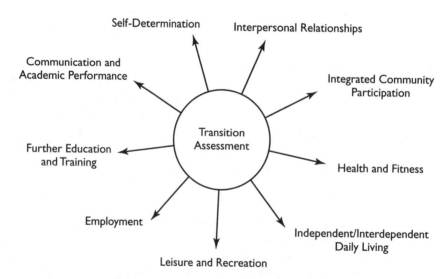

Figure 3.1. Knowledge and skill domains for transition assessment. (From SITLINGTON, PATRICIA L.; CLARK, GARY M., TRANSITION EDUCATION AND SERVICES FOR STUDENTS WITH DISABILITIES, 4th Edition, © 2006, p. 134. Reprinted by permission of Pearson Education, Inc., Upper Saddle River, NJ.)

1. What do I already know about this student that would be helpful in developing postsecondary outcomes?

2. What information do I need to know about this individual to determine postsecondary goals?

3. What methods will provide this information?

4. How will the assessment data be collected and used in the IEP process?

Figure 3.2. Transition assessment planning form. (From KOCHHAR-BRYANT, CAROL A., GREENE, GARY A., PATHWAYS TO SUCCESSFUL TRANSITION FOR YOUTH WITH DISABILITLIES: A DEVELOPMENTAL PROCESS, 2nd Edition, © 2009. Reprinted by permission of Pearson Education, Upper Saddle River, NJ.)

and academic skills, behavior characteristics, work skills, family background, values and beliefs) and various environments in which the individual may participate after completing high school (college, vocational training school, work, life). The purpose of this analysis is to determine whether a potential match exists between the individual and the environments to which he or she may make the transition in the future. For example, a youth with a disability who has significant support needs may not be a good match for a 4-year university bachelor's degree program. However, this individual may be a good match for a supported work environment or supported living environment. The Making the Match transition assessment model analysis yields one of three possible conclusions: 1) yes, a match exists; 2) possibly, a match exists; or 3) no, a match does not exist. The model identifies various options for special education and transition personnel to consider in determining how to proceed with transition planning (see options in the box Is There a Match? in Figure 3.3).

One final transition assessment resource to consider is the Iowa Model for Transition Assessments, developed by the Iowa Department of Education and available online (http://transitionassessment.northcentralrrc.org). This ongoing, coordinated, systematic process

1. Collects/gathers relevant (appropriate) information/data on a student's interests, preferences, strengths and needs as they relate to the student's postsecondary expectations for living, learning, and working
2. Begins at least by the year the student turns 14 years of age and continues until the student graduates or ages out
3. Provides data from which to plan and make decisions that assist the student to move to postsecondary activities of living, learning, and working
4. Involves input from student, family, school personnel, and other relevant stakeholders such as adult agencies, related services personnel (the IEP team; "Iowa Model for Transition Assessments," n.d.)

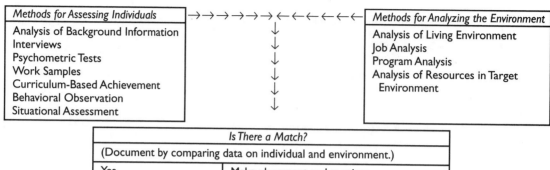

Methods for Assessing Individuals		Methods for Analyzing the Environment
Analysis of Background Information Interviews Psychometric Tests Work Samples Curriculum-Based Achievement Behavioral Observation Situational Assessment		Analysis of Living Environment Job Analysis Program Analysis Analysis of Resources in Target Environment

Is There a Match?	
(Document by comparing data on individual and environment.)	
Yes	Make placement and monitor.
Possibly	Identify supports needed. Identify accommodations needed. Identify instruction needed.
No	Continue to collect data on other environments. Continue to collect data on the individual. Initiate matching process again.

Figure 3.3. Making the Match transition assessment model. (From Sitlington, P.L., Neubert, D.A., Begun, W., Lombard, R.C., & Leconte, P.J. [1996]. *Assess for success: Handbook on transition assessment* [p. 99]. Arlington, VA: Council for Exceptional Children; reprinted by permission.)

The process for determining the individual transition needs of a youth with a disability requires the IEP team to answer the following questions:

1. Does the student have a postsecondary expectation in each one or more of the following areas: living, learning, and working?
2. What are the essential understandings, habits, attitudes, and skills that any individual needs for these postsecondary expectations?
3. What are this student's current attitudes, habits, basic skills, and critical thinking and application skills?
4. What is the discrepancy between the essential skills and the student's current skills? ("Iowa Model for Transition Assessments," n.d.)

The Iowa Transition Assessment web site contains a total of 12 cells with transition assessment instruments that professionals can use to obtain information related to these questions, organized by the categories Living, Learning, and Working. Similar to the process outlined in the Making the Match transition assessment model, the IEP team can use the information obtained from these assessments to determine a student's interests, current level of basic skills, and any possible discrepancy between the two. The IEP team can subsequently proceed in planning instruction, supports, and activities when developing an IEP or transition IEP for the student. Some topics of the Transition Planning Assessment Area: Cell 4 (Home and Community Living Skills) from the web site are shown in Table 3.1.

Before turning to transition assessment information recommended for an SOP, I present a brief case study of a CLD youth with a disability who has completed high school to illustrate the importance of an SOP and the assessment information that it can potentially provide.

Table 3.1. Sample topic of the Transition Planning Assessment Area

Transition Planning Assessment Areas	What are we assessing?	How can you assess it and how can you access the suggested data collection or assessment sources?
Cell 4: Home and Community Living Skills	Home and community living skills needed to perform daily living skills activities	Review student files or portfolios to see if any home and community living skills have been documented from any previous assessment effort.
		Interview student to elicit self-evaluation of those daily living skills and adult community living skills that are most related to the student's postsecondary goals for living situation preferences. Interview format may be brief with direct questions related to the type and location of living situations.
		Conduct formal or informal observations of the student performing daily living and adult community living sills. Document observations in the student's file or portfolio. Many of these are difficult to obtain in the home or community, but simulated task observations at school may be a reasonable alternative (e.g., meal preparation, budgeting)
		Conduct community-based situational assessment of life skills and community living skills. This type of assessment is most easily performed within settings that permit skills demonstrations, such as school environments containing kitchens, living areas, and bath areas or off-campus units in apartments, houses, or other home-like environments. Formats for assessing and documenting skills may include checklists or rating scales. An example of a checklist instrument is from Informal Assessments for Transition Planning (IATP), Comprehensive Inventory of Transition Knowledge and Kills, Items 12–16, pp. 18–22. Another example in one area of daily living is Assessment of Financial Sills and Abilities, also from IAPT, p. 108. Either or both of these may be used as informal assessment instruments independent of a community-based situational assessment. IATP (Clark, Patton, & Moulton, 2000) is published by PRO-ED, Inc., 8700 Shoal Creek Blvd., Austin, TX 78757, www.proedinc.com

From *Iowa Model Transition Matrix: Methods and tools. Home and community living skills* (n.d.). Retrieved Feb. 7, 2011, from http://transition assessment.northcentralrrc.org/cell4.aspx. Des Moines, IA: Iowa Transition Assessment; reprinted by permission.

 **Qui Tran's SOP**

Qui Tran is a 19-year-old Vietnamese young woman who has graduated high school with a diploma. She has a diagnosis of a learning disability and ADHD, and although she is happy and excited to be out of high school, has no idea what to do now. She has been living at home with her parents but has not engaged in any purposeful activity (e.g., postsecondary education, employment, vocational training) during the day. She has been unable to find a job, and her mother does not know what to do. She wants Qui to do something outside of the home but is also fearful of her being out in the community because of safety concerns. Another parent of a youth with a disability from Qui's high school suggested to Mrs. Tran that she and Qui meet with a counselor at the Department of Vocational Rehabilitation (VR). Mrs. Tran followed her advice and set up an appointment.

The VR counselor told Mrs. Tran that Qui is not automatically entitled to receive services but that her eligibility for the VR program must be determined. This would require a series of tests. Mrs. Tran was hesitant to put Qui through such a lengthy process because of her daughter's short attention span and the difficulty she has experienced with taking assessments in the past. The counselor asked Mrs. Tran whether she had copies of the assessment results from Qui's high school years in special education. Mrs. Tran said that she did not but believed that these were available, having remembered that an SOP was created for Qui just before she had graduated from high school. The VR counselor told Mrs. Tran that if she could bring him that document, it would save a lot of time and speed up the process of determining whether Qui was eligible for VR services and which services would be appropriate. Mrs. Tran thanked the counselor and said that she would get Qui's SOP from the high school and return to meet with him soon.

The case study of Qui Tran illustrates the importance of the transition assessment information contained in an SOP, which can be used to help determine eligibility for disability-related services after a youth with a disability completes high school. Before I discuss the specifics of the assessment data in an SOP, it is appropriate to provide a brief history of this document.

Kochhar-Bryant and Izzo's (2006) article on SOPs presents a thorough background on the history and legal requirements of this document. At the time of their article's publication, minimal implementation guidelines about SOPs had been provided to states in IDEA 2004 requirements. Beginning in 2003 and for up to 2 years afterward, a collaborative group of transition-related stakeholders (i.e., secondary and postsecondary representatives, rehabilitation specialists, consumer advocates, and parents) met and worked on identifying SOP implementation recommendations. These individuals formed the National Transition Documentation Summit "to develop an SOP that would bridge the documentation gap between (a) IDEA and (b) Section 504 of the Rehabilitation Act and the [Americans with Disabilities Act] while meeting the needs of students/consumers and their adult service providers" (Kochhar-Bryant & Izzo, 2006, p. 72). The group also met with several national disability-related organizations, such as the Learning Disabilities Association of America, the Higher Education Consortium for Special Education, the Council for Exceptional Children, and the DCDT. The summit representatives crafted a model SOP template in response to the input, guidance, and feedback they received from the field. This was possible because neither IDEA nor the U.S. Department of Education had mandated a specific format or content for an SOP, and thus local education organizations had the flexibility to develop their own SOPs. The sample SOP template developed by the National Transition Documentation Summit (2005) appears as Figure 3.10 (for Qui Tran), and a blank copy can be found in the chapter appendix. The SOP template is made up of five parts and should be completed by the student's case

Neither IDEA nor the U.S. Department of Education has mandated a specific format or content for an SOP.

manager with substantial input from the student and his or her IEP team. Part 1, Background Information, includes demographic information and the student's disability diagnosis, and it is to this section that recent evaluations and assessments should be attached. If possible, the data should come from multiple, culturally responsive assessment tools. Part 2 lists the student's postsecondary goals, indicating the settings in which he or she will be participating after high school in terms of education, employment, and independent living. Qui Tran and her family, for example, agreed that her goals included enrolling in a vocational training program and obtaining part-time employment in the fashion industry while continuing to live at home with her family. Part 3 of the template, titled Summary of Performance, provides spaces to indicate the student's present level of performance in academic, cognitive, and functional areas. This summary should be supported by data, but may have slightly different emphases depending on a student's postsecondary goals. For example, if a student is aiming to pursue postsecondary education, it is particularly important to include thorough data for the academic content areas (Dukes, 2010). Next to the spaces where a present level of performance is indicated, there is space to provide information on the essential accommodations, modifications, or assistive technology used in high school by the youth with a disability and why these are needed.

Completing the SOP provides an opportunity to analyze a student's data and discuss with the family and team how that data illustrates the student's strengths and needs and what that all means in relation to the student's goals. Part 4 of the SOP is where these ideas are synthesized—a space is provided for Recommendations to Assist the Student in Meeting Postsecondary Goals. Because eligibility requirements are very different in post-school settings, what is written here can be considered suggestions only, no matter how essential certain accommodations and services have seemed to be through high school. Nevertheless, this document is a valuable tool that can be shared with others to substantiate a youth's request for a certain accommodation or service, and it also enables the student to advocate more effectively for him or herself by knowing what strategies and supports have helped in the past. Indeed, the final part of the SOP is a section for the student to complete, reflecting on the impact of his or her disability and what accommodations and services have been the most helpful. This part is optional but highly recommended, and when working with CLD youth it can be especially useful for ensuring that the student's voice is heard.

It is also necessary to include transition assessment information in a transition IEP. Most transition IEPs have spaces for entering data on the student's present level of performance in various areas (i.e., instruction, community experiences, employment, adult living, and, when appropriate, daily living skills and functional vocational evaluation) written in the transition services language requirements stated in IDEA 2004. Similar to SOPs, IDEA and the U.S. Department of Education do not require states to use a specific transition IEP format but rather allow local school districts to develop their own. Hence, transition IEP formats vary greatly from state to state transition IEP from school district to school district. A sample transition IEP format taken from Kochhar-Bryant and Greene (2009) appears in the chapter appendix. It contains a large space for current level of performance data (i.e., transition assessment results).

Transition IEP formats vary greatly from state to state and from school district to school district.

WHAT TYPES OF TRANSITION PROGRAMS AND SERVICES ARE AVAILABLE IN HIGH SCHOOL AND BEYOND THAT MEET THE NEEDS OF CLD FAMILIES AND YOUTH WITH DISABILITIES?

A multitude of transition programs and services are available for CLD families and youth with disabilities during high school and after the youths graduate from or complete high school. Special education teachers, school psychologists, counselors, speech-language therapists, assistive technology specialists, nurses, adaptive physical education teachers, and occupational therapists are the primary individuals involved in providing school-based transition supports and services to high school youth with disabilities. In addition, many school districts employ transition specialists who focus on 1) overseeing employment development for youth with disabilities, 2) helping youth with disabilities obtain paid work in the community while they are in high school, and 3) connecting youth with disabilities to adult transition service agencies. All school-based transition personnel should possess critical knowledge and skills for working with CLD families and youth with disabilities. The assessment instrument presented in the Chapter 2 appendix allows transition personnel to determine their level of skills and knowledge. Culturally responsive collaboration training in transition services and supports should be provided to all school-based transition personnel who lack this critical knowledge and skills (see Chapter 2 for specific training recommendations).

One of the key transition planning decisions that all families and youth with disabilities face in high school is selecting a course of study. IDEA 1997 included the selection of a high school course of study beginning at age 14 as a transition requirement for youth with disabilities; however, this was changed in 2004 when the required age for transition once again became when the student turns 16, as had been the case for IDEA 1990. Choosing a course of study to pursue in high school is an important decision that influences the types of transition services and supports the youth with a disability is entitled to receive during the high school years.

Choosing a course of study to pursue in high school is an important decision that influences the types of transition services and supports the youth with a disability is entitled to receive during the high school years.

A helpful resource for determining needed transition services and supports in high school is the Pathways to Successful Transition Model created by Kochhar-Bryant & Greene (Greene & Kochhar-Bryant, 2003; Kochhar Bryant & Greene, 2009), shown in Table 3.2. The model displays four pathways (high school course of study options) that correspond to IDEA 2004 transition services language requirements (i.e., instruction, community experiences, employment and other postsecondary adult living objectives, functional vocational evaluation and daily living skills). The pathways are noncategorical and can apply to any youth with a disability. However, the level and intensity of transition services and supports increases with each successive pathway. For example, a youth with a disability who selects Pathway 1 and is interested in employment might need some initial help with prevocational skills, job search skills, and an employment search but should be able to function fully independently once he or she obtains employment. A student who selects Pathway 4, in contrast, will probably need ongoing support in employment development, training, and on-the-job assistance throughout the entire employment process. Other examples of differences in the intensity of transition services and supports can be seen in terms of instruction as well as community experiences. Instruction for Pathway 1 consists of a fully inclusive high school college preparatory course of study leading to passage of the high school exit exam, obtainment of a diploma, and entrance into a 2-year college or 4-year university. Instruction for Pathway 4, in contrast, consists of a semi-inclusive high school curriculum emphasizing functional academics, social skills, and life skills leading to the obtainment of a high school certificate of completion (not a diploma) and entrance into community-based competitive or supported employment. Community experiences are not needed for Pathway 1 because youth pursuing this course of study are often able to function fully independently in the community. Students pursuing Pathway 4, however, usually need community-based instruction

Table 3.2. Pathways to Successful Transition Model from Kochhar-Bryant and Greene (2009)

PATHWAY I

The youth with disabilities will (a) participate in a fully integrated high school college preparatory curriculum lead-ing to passage of high school exit exam, obtainment of a standard high school diploma, and entrance into a 2- or 4-year college or university, (b) function fully independently in the community, (c) complete career exploration activities and paid work experiences in high school, (d) obtain a college degree that leads to full-time competi-tive employment with salary and benefits, and (e) live fully independently as an adult.

PATHWAY 2

The youth with disabilities will (a) participate in a fully integrated high school curriculum of blended career and vocational courses leading to passage of high school exit exam with necessary accommodations, obtainment of a standard high school diploma, and entrance into a vocational-technical school or career apprenticeship, (b) func-tion fully independently in the community, including independent living, (c) complete career exploration and paid work experience in high school, and (d) obtain full-time competitive employment with salary and possible bene-fits in their career interest.

PATHWAY 3

The youth with disabilities will (a) participate in a semi-integrated high school curriculum of blended career and vocational courses leading to obtainment of a high school certificate of completion and entrance into community-based paid competitive employment with time-limited supports, (b) function semi-independently in the commu-nity with necessary supports, (c) obtain functional daily living skills needed for full or semi-independent living, (d) participate in a functional vocational evaluation that identifies competitive employment skills, and (e) partici-pate in integrated paid competitive employment with necessary supports.

PATHWAY 4

The youth with disabilities will (a) participate in a semi-integrated high school curriculum emphasizing functional academics, social skills, life skills, self-determination and self-advocacy skills leading to obtainment of a high school certificate of completion and entrance into community-based competitive or supported employment, (b) function semi-independently in the community with necessary supports, (c) obtain daily living skills needed for independent or supported living, (d) participate in a functional vocational evaluation that identifies competitive employment skills, and (e) participate in community-based competitive or supported employment.

From Kochhar-Bryant, C.A., & Greene, G. (2009). *Pathways to successful transition for youth with disabilities: A developmental process* (2nd ed.). Upper Saddle River, NJ: Merrill/Pearson; reprinted by permission.

and supports throughout their high school years in order to learn to function semi-independently in the community.

Various transition services personnel are associated with the four pathways contained in the model. Pathway 1 personnel typically include RSP professionals, paraprofessionals, a career specialist, a college counselor, and an employment specialist. Pathway 4 transition personnel usually include a special day class teacher, paraprofessionals, a community-based instructor (who might also be the special day class teacher), an adaptive physical education teacher, an occupational therapist, an orientation and mobility training specialist, a supported employment specialist, and possibly a supported living specialist. Again, all of these individuals should possess essential knowledge and skills for collaborating in culturally responsive ways with CLD families and youth with disabilities; training should be provided to those who do not.

A number of important community-based as well as state and federal transition service agencies exist to provide needed assistance to individuals with disabilities after they graduate from or complete high school. The California Department of Education (2007) published *Transition to Adult Living: An Information and Resource Guide,* which lists relevant agencies found in the state of California, many of which also exist nationwide (see Figure 3.4). The matrixes show the name of

A number of important community-based, state, and federal transition service agencies exist to provide assistance to individuals with disabilities after they graduate from or complete high school.

Interagency/Community-Based Matrix

Resources: Interagency or Community-Based	Education	Occupational/Technical Skills	Career Guidance/Research	Transition Assistance/Case Management	Employment Services	Financial Assistance	Counseling Services	Drug and Alcohol Counseling	Health/Mental Health Benefits	Supported Employment, Living Services	Community Access	Recreation
Apprenticeship	X	X	X			X						
Trade School	X	X	X		X	X						
Community College	X	X	X	X	X	X	X					
University System	X	X	X	X		X	X					
Parks and Recreation												X
Community Events												X
Community Ed	X											X
YMCA												X
Public Transportation											X	
EDD*			X									
One Stop Career Ctr		X	X	X	X							
WIA*	X	X	X	X	X	X	X	X		X		
Private Employment										X		
Employers				X					X	X		

State Matrix

State and Federal Agencies	Education	Occupational/Technical Skills	Career Guidance/Research	Transition Assistance/Case Management	Employment Services	Financial Assistance	Counseling Services	Drug and Alcohol Counseling	Health/Mental Health Benefits	Supported Employment, Living Services	Community Access	Recreation
Dept. of Rehab.	X	X	X	X	X	X	X	X		X		
DDS*: Regional Ctr				X						X	X	X
Social Security						X			X			
Mental Health							X	X				
Employment Development Department		X	X	X	X		X					

*Acronyms
    EDD: Employment Development Department
    WIA: Workforce Investment Act
    DDS: Department of Developmental Services

Figure 3.4. Matrixes showing examples of agencies providing transition services in the state of California. (From California Department of Education. [2007]. *Transition to adult living: An information and resource guide* [p. 73]. Sacramento, CA: Author; reprinted by permission.)

the agency and the type of transition services and supports it offers. The majority of these agencies are committed to providing culturally responsive transition services and supports to youth and adults with disabilities and have well-trained personnel who possess essential knowledge and skills for interacting with CLD families and youth and adults with disabilities. Check the Internet to find one of these agencies in your area.

A key transition support for CLD youth with disabilities who elect to enter a 2-year college or 4-year university is Disability Support Services (DSS). All colleges and universities are required by the Americans with Disabilities Act (ADA) of 1990 (PL 101-336) to provide assistance to enrolled students with disabilities who are determined eligible to receive these services. Note that eligibility for these services often must be independently determined by DSS personnel; an enrolled student who received special education services in high school does not automatically qualify for DSS services in higher education. Moreover, these services are governed by laws other than IDEA (i.e., Section 504 of the Rehabilitation Act Amendments of 1998 [PL 105-220]; ADA of 1990). However, CLD youth with disabilities who possess an SOP and provide this document to DSS personnel are likely to be determined eligible to receive college support services. DSS services available at many colleges and universities in the United States include

- Notetakers
- Extended time on tests
- Access to assistive technology
- Stress management and other personal counseling services
- Assistance with class selection and enrollment
- Help with study skills
- Help with time management and organizational skills
- Self-advocacy training

These types of transition supports and services are invaluable and frequently can make the difference between individuals with disabilities successfully completing college or dropping out from school early in their college careers.

The following case study presents culturally responsive transition programming in high school. This is followed by specific examples of culturally responsive transition IEPs and SOPs.

A key transition support for CLD youth with disabilities who elect to enter a 2-year college or 4-year university is Disability Support Services.

Cho Hee Dan's High School Course of Study

When Cho Hee Dan first entered middle school at age 12, one of the things discussed at her IEP meeting was the type of special education program and services she and her parents would select when she makes the transition to high school. When Cho Hee was in eighth grade, the IEP team chose to revisit this question.

Cho Hee had been in special day classes throughout her school years, and though this continued to be an option in high school, the special education staff wanted to determine the course of study that would best meet her needs and reflect the desires and wishes of her family. One of the recommendations the middle school IEP team made to Cho Hee and her family prior to the eighth-grade IEP meeting was to visit the high school she would be attending, talk to the special education teachers there, and speak to a few other CLD families of youth with disabilities about their child's high school program and experiences. There was a Korean special education support group in the district with whom the Dans could connect. These action items were included in Cho Hee's seventh-grade IEP. In addition, the special education team provided the Dan family with a copy of the Pathways to Successful Transition Model for the parents to review, discuss, and consider as they explored high school course of study options for their daughter.

The Dans followed all of the recommendations of the middle school IEP team and were anxious to share their thoughts at the eighth-grade IEP meeting. Mr. Dan was not able to attend the meeting, but Mrs. Dan felt comfortable speaking for both of them.

Mrs. Dan said the following when asked about the course of study Cho Hee should pursue in high school: "My husband and I think that Cho Hee still needs to be in a special day class because this is best for her. We do want her to make friends with other children in high school and be in some activities with them, such as going to football games to watch her older brother play or taking some classes with the other students. We talked with some other families in the Korean special education support group and visited the high school special education program with Cho Hee. She likes the high school special day class teacher and the classroom activities. The families we talked to said this would be a good program for Cho Hee."

Cho Hee's middle school special day class teacher, who was attending the IEP meeting, asked Mrs. Dan whether her family wanted Cho Hee to earn her high school diploma. Mrs. Dan replied, "We are not sure that is the most important thing for her. She has been learning basic life skills in middle school, and my husband and I want this type of program to continue in high school. Many of the families we talked to say the high school special day class is very good at teaching these skills and helping the children become more independent. We like this idea. Also, they told us that there is a 'Best Buddies' program at the high school that pairs students with disabilities with peers without disabilities to help with friendships and activities. Cho Hee is very excited about this and wants to participate in the Best Buddies program!"

The middle school special day class teacher then asked Mrs. Dan whether she had looked at the Pathways to Successful Transition Model and talked this over with her family. Mrs. Dan responded, "Yes, and we all think that Pathway 3 sounds like the right one for Cho Hee." The middle school special day class teacher said that this was also the opinion of the IEP team. The IEP team would use a Pathway 3 course of study to write the goals and objectives for the current IEP. This would include career exploration activities for Cho Hee in high school and a functional career and life skills assessment to help determine possible job placements for her during her high school years. In addition, the transition specialist at the high school would work with the high school special day class teacher to provide community-based instruction for Cho Hee to help her learn how to get around and access various places in the community of interest to her. Finally, the middle school special day class teacher told Mrs. Dan that the high school special day class teacher and transition specialist would conduct transition assessments with Cho Hee and the family shortly after she begins high school and use this information to write transition IEP goals when Cho Hee turns 16.

The meeting ended with Mrs. Dan stating that she and her husband were very pleased with the program and services Cho Hee had received in middle school and that they looked forward to their daughter starting high school next year.

WHAT ARE EXAMPLES OF QUALITY, CULTURALLY RESPONSIVE TRANSITION IEPs AND SOPs?

This section discusses sample transition IEPs and an SOP that reflect culturally responsive transition assessment and planning. A number of important things must occur and be in place in order to ensure the likelihood of creating culturally responsive transition IEPs and SOPs, summarized in a checklist format in Figure 3.5. Special education and transition personnel should utilize this checklist to evaluate and improve, if indicated, the quality of culturally responsive transition IEPs and SOPs that exist in their school districts.

Consider the sample transition IEP for Juan Carlos Martinez, whose case study appears earlier in this chapter. Figure 3.6 shows the transition assessment data corresponding to the components of the Making the Match transition assessment model by Sitlington et al. (1996); it includes assessment information on Juan Carlos and on potential transition environments. A corresponding transition IEP for Juan Carlos that contains many of these transition assessment data is shown in Figure 3.7. A blank form appears in the appendix.

The sample transition IEP for Juan Carlos Martinez contains important transition assessment data in several locations. Juan Carlos's and his family's vision for his future is displayed in the Vision box. This vision includes earning a high school diploma; taking art education classes in high school, vocational school, or college; working in an art-related job; and living fully independently in the community. These goals were discussed and agreed upon with his family at the meeting held at their house with Mr. Jimenez, Juan Carlos's RSP teacher. Other relevant individual assessment information appears in the Career Interests box (e.g., Art, Drawing, Illustration) and the Strengths box (e.g., Good work habits, Good social skills, Bilingual in English and Spanish). The Present Level of Performance box contains individual transition assessment data on Juan Carlos that summarize his current academic performance (i.e., cognitive and academic functioning) and capabilities in the areas of community, employment, and postsecondary training and learning. Transition environment assessment data are summarized in this section of the transition IEP as well (i.e., environments in which Juan Carlos functions fully independently and in which he is capable of participating). The Transition Service Needs box contains statements about the transition supports Juan Carlos requires in order to be successful in school, employment, and postsecondary education environments (e.g., RSP support, prevocational training, job development, job placement, DSS supports at community college or university). The Needed Transition Services box lists the specific transition services Juan Carlos will receive in high school and after graduating from high school (e.g., RSP support, prevocational classes, art classes, ELL services, and DSS services in college). Finally, the Transition Goals box contains goals written in the transition services language requirements of IDEA 2004. These goals correspond to the statements contained in the Pathways to Successful Transition Model (in this instance primarily Pathway 2). Note that these goals do not contain all of the components required of goals in an IEP, such as starting dates, behaviors, evaluation method and criteria, people responsible, or benchmarks. Rather, these transition goals are written as broad, general statements, as permitted in IDEA 2004. Kochhar-Bryant and Greene (2009) recommended that the components missing in the transition goals be written into an accompanying IEP that corresponds to the broad transition IEP goals. Because of space limitations, an accompanying IEP of this type for Juan Carlos is not provided here.

A case study, transition assessment information, and sample transition IEP for a CLD youth with a disability pursuing Pathway 4 are presented next.

Checklist for Writing Culturally Responsive Transition IEPs and SOPs

____ All special education and transition personnel involved in writing transition IEPs and SOPs have been administered the CLD Transition Knowledge and Skill Evaluation Instrument.

____ All special education and transition personnel involved in writing transition IEPs and SOPs possess *good* to *excellent* CLD transition knowledge and skills.

____ A variety of culturally responsive transition assessments and methods have been used to gather transition information about the CLD youth with a disability.

____ A variety of people have participated in the transition assessment process, including the CLD family and youth with a disability.

____ The transition assessment process has looked at a variety of future transition environments for the CLD youth with a disability.

____ The Pathways to Successful Transition Model has been shared and discussed with the CLD family and youth with a disability.

____ The IEP team has utilized the transition assessment data to engage in person-centered transition planning with the CLD youth with a disability and his or her family.

____ The transition IEP or SOP contains all of the following sections and relevant transition information about the CLD youth with a disability:

a. Present levels of performance

b. Interests, needs, and preferences related to the transition services language requirements of IDEA 2004

c. Postsecondary goals corresponding to the transition language service requirements of IDEA 2004

d. Designation of transition personnel, programs, or agencies that will provide the needed transition services to meet the transition IEP goals

e. Action steps and dates of expected completion of the transition IEP goals (see IEP page)

f. Signatures of all individuals who participated in the transition IEP meeting and agreed or disagreed with the transition IEP goals (see IEP page)

Figure 3.5. Checklist for writing culturally responsive transition IEPs and SOPs. (*Key:* CLD, culturally and linguistically diverse; IEP, individualized education program; IDEA, Individuals with Disabilities Education Act.)

Individual assessment information for Juan Carlos Martinez:
- 11th grade, 16-year-old Mexican American male
- Specific learning disability in language processing
- Cognitive functioning in the average range
- Sixth-grade level academic functioning in reading, math, writing, and spelling
- Speaks Spanish at home; receives English language learner support in school
- Mother and father and three younger siblings living in home
- Lower socioeconomic status
- Enrolled in general education classes with Resource Specialist Program (RSP) support
- Capable of passing high school exit exam and earning high school diploma with RSP support
- Good behavior and social skills
- Has several friends in school
- Talent and capability in drawing and art
- Interested in art vocational training, postsecondary art education, and art as a possible future career

---

Transition environment assessment data for Juan Carlos Martinez:
- Functions fully independently in the home environment and performs most daily living skills proficiently
- Functions fully independently in the community
- Successfully participates in general education classrooms with RSP support services and accommodations
- Has good work habits and completes most tasks in a timely manner both in school and at home
- Has good potential for successful participation and completion of art education classes in high school, vocational school, or postsecondary education settings
- Capable of successful participation in paid employment in the community
- Transition support services available for job development and training in the community

---

Figure 3.6.   Individual and transition environment assessment data for Juan Carlos Martinez.

James Montgomery's Transition IEP Meeting

James Montgomery is a 16-year-old African American young man with a moderate to severe disability. He has a developmental disability and functions in the low average cognitive range, with limited language and communication skills. He functions academically around a first-grade level in most subjects. He has some degree of independence in self-care and requires varying degrees of support in order to function at home, in school, and in the community. He has been enrolled in special education throughout his school years and is currently in a high school special day class that focuses on basic academics, daily living skills, and community-based instruction. One full-time special day class teacher and three paraprofessionals work with him and the other students in the classroom. James's

Vision
- High school diploma
- Art education in high school, vocational school, college
- Work in art-related job
- Live fully independently in the community

Career interests
- Art
- Drawing
- Illustration
- Graphic design

Strengths
- Good work habits
- Good social skills
- Bilingual in English and Spanish
- Motivated to succeed
- Positive family relationships

Present level of performance

Academics: Cognitive functioning is in the average range; academic functioning at the sixth-grade level in reading, writing, spelling, and math (see IEP present levels of performance for specific cognitive and achievement data, grade-level equivalents, and standard scores)

Community: Functions fully independently in the community. Has a driver's license and is capable of transporting himself independently by car in the community.

Employment: Is capable of working fully independently in paid employment. Needs prevocational training, vocational training, and paid work experience.

Postsecondary training and learning: Is capable of participating in vocational training or postsecondary education training in an art-related field or career.

Transition service needs
- Juan Carlos requires RSP support in general education classes and for one period a day in the RSP classroom.
- Juan Carlos needs support from a transition specialist to help with prevocational training, job development, and job placement.
- Juan Carlos will need assistance from DSS to be successful in classes in community college or university.

Needed transition services

Instruction: RSP support and accommodations in general education classes.

Community: None needed.

Employment: Juan Carlos will participate in prevocational training classes and art classes in high school and postsecondary education.

Related services: Juan Carlos will receive ELL services through completion of high school; DSS services in college.

Daily living: None needed.

Functional vocational evaluation: Not needed.

Transition goals

Instruction: Fully inclusive high school curriculum of blended career and vocational courses leading to passage of high school exit exam with necessary accommodations, obtainment of a standard high school diploma, and entrance into a vocational-technical school, career apprenticeship, or 2- or 4-year college or university.

Community: Function fully independently in the community.

Employment and other postschool adult living objectives: Career exploration and paid work experience in high school; vocational-technical school or career apprenticeship-based full-time competitive employment with salary and possible benefits; independent living as an adult.

Supplementary and related services: Juan will maintain a minimum grade point average of 3.00 with the help of RSP in all college-preparatory classes in high school and will obtain academic support and assistance from DSS at community college or university.

Figure 3.7.   Individualized transition plan for Juan Carlos Martinez. (*Key:* IEP, individualized education program; RSP, Resource Specialist Program; ELL, English language learner; DSS, Disability Support Services. *Source:* Kochhar-Bryant and Greene [2009])

classroom is located at his neighborhood high school; he is included in some elective classes on campus, receives adaptive physical education, but spends the majority of his day in the special day class.

The transition specialist recently completed a transition assessment for James using the Iowa Model for Transition Assessments. Though more transition data are needed in the future, the information obtained from the initial assessment was used to draft transition IEP goals for James. The transition assessment process involved multiple sources of data, including input from James's family on goals for his future.

Figure 3.8 shows the results of the transition assessment, and Figure 3.9 shows the transition IEP developed for James. The sample transition IEP for James reflects the thoughts of James, his parents, and school special education and transition personnel. The assessment data were based on the Iowa Model for Transition Assessments and reflected James's postsecondary interests, preferences, and strengths in the categories of living, learning, and working. The transition IEP developed for James contains these transition assessment data throughout (Vision, Career Interests, Strengths, Present Level of Performance, Transition Service Needs, Needed Transition Services, and Transition Goals). Special education and transition services personnel used the assessment data to draft transition goals for James that correspond to Pathway 4 in the Pathways to Successful Transition Model. A key decision by James's family is to enroll him in an adult transition program at age 18 so that he can continue to receive special education and transition services from the school district until

---

Transition Assessment

1. *Student profile:* 16-year-old, African American male; developmental disability; low average cognitive skills, first-grade academic skills; language and communication skills at first-grade level; limited self-help skills, needs support in many daily living skills such as eating, dressing, bathing, and hygiene; good social skills, gets along well with peers and adults.
2. *Student's postsecondary interests, preferences, and strengths:*
   a. *Living:* James prefers that he live at home with his family, as do his parents. Parents expressed a desire for James to develop better daily living skills so that he can function more independently in the home and out in the community.
   b. *Learning:* James needs to learn daily living skills in the areas of self-help and personal care, "stranger danger" training, orientation and mobility training that includes the use of public transportation, and community awareness and access.
   c. *Working:* James needs to participate in a functional vocational evaluation that will determine his work capabilities. He is good at working with his hands and is a good candidate for supported employment.
3. *Summary of input from student, family, school and transition personnel:*
   James's family plans to have James live at home but desires that he become more independent in his self-care and daily living skills. They want James to participate in activities in the community during the day to prevent boredom and inappropriate behavior. His parents are considering that James not complete high school at age 18 but instead be placed in the school district's 18- to 22-year-old adult transition class. This class will allow James the opportunity to continue receiving special education services in his areas of need, such as job development and supported employment. His parents are also in favor of this placement because the class is on an inclusive college campus in the community where James would be surrounded by peers without disabilities; have access to elective classes of interest to him; and be provided with paraprofessional support in class, on campus, and out in the community. The individualized education program recommends the adult transition class as a future environment that would be a good match for James. The team also recommends that James explore his eligibility for vocational rehabilitation services after he turns 18. A Summary of Functional Performance document will be completed when James exits the school district program.

Figure 3.8.   Transition assessment for James Montgomery.

Vision
- Adult transition class
- Certificate of completion
- Semi-independent functioning in the community
- Supported employment

Career interests
- Movies and media
- Construction trades

Strengths
- Is good working with his hands
- Is friendly and has good social skills
- Follows directions well
- Is able to focus attention when task is of interest to him

Present level of performance

Academics: Functions in the low average cognitive range; academic functioning at first-grade level in reading, writing, spelling and math (see IEP present levels of performance for specific cognitive and achievement data, grade-level equivalents, and standard scores).

Community: Not able to function independently in the community at the present time. Needs community-based instruction to develop semi-independent functioning in the community in the future.

Employment: Has not developed employment skills at the present time. Needs to complete a functional vocational evaluation to determine employment capabilities and skills. Is interested in working.

Postsecondary training and learning: Capable of participating in supported employment and accessing community semi-independently. Possible candidate for supported living in the future.

Transition service needs
- James needs to develop daily living skills, orientation and mobility skills, and community awareness and access.
- James needs to develop employment skills for possible future supported employment.
- James needs to develop independent living skills for possible future supported living.

Needed transition services

Instruction: Special day class in high school and Adult Transition Program at age 18.

Community: Community-based instruction.

Employment: Functional vocational evaluation and supported employment placement.

Related services: Transition employment specialist; VR counselor.

Daily living: Supported living specialist.

Transition goals

Instruction: Participate in semi-inclusive high school curriculum emphasizing functional academics, social skills, life skills, self-determination, and self-advocacy skills leading to obtainment of a high school certificate of completion and entrance into community-based competitive or supported employment.

Community: Function semi-independently in the community with necessary supports; obtain daily living skills needed for independent or supported living.

Employment: Participate in a functional vocational evaluation that identifies competitive employment skills; participate in community-based competitive or supported employment.

Supplementary and related services: Transition specialist to complete functional vocational evaluation with James and explore supported employment opportunities that match James's vocational interests and capabilities; VR services at age 18.

Figure 3.9. Individualized transition plan for James Montgomery. (*Key:* IEP, individualized education program; VR, vocational rehabilitation. *Source:* Kochar-Bryant and Greene [2009])

age 22. This will allow James to further develop essential skills in academics, daily living, community functioning, and employment under the support and supervision of well-trained transition services personnel. Moreover, it offers James the opportunity to leave the high school environment and make the transition to a more age-appropriate environment (e.g., a community college campus) in the future. His parents' satisfaction with the transition goals and future placements is evidence that they and the IEP team engaged in effective and culturally responsive collaboration.

This final case study revisits Qui Tran, the 19-year-old Vietnamese woman who has graduated high school with a diploma. Recall that in her previous case study, her mother needed to obtain Qui's SOP (see Figure 3.10) for the VR counselor in order to qualify her daughter for VR services. The following case study demonstrates how having the SOP helped the VR counselor determine the appropriate adult transition services for Qui Tran.

Mrs. Tran's Return Visit to the VR Counselor

Mrs. Tran returned to visit the VR counselor and provided him with a copy of Qui's SOP from high school. The VR counselor reviewed the document and said that it contained all of the important information he was looking for and that Qui does qualify for VR services. He said to Mrs. Tran, "Pardon me for asking, but is there a reason you didn't bring me this when you came to visit me last time?" Mrs. Tran said that she did not know what this document was for and did not remember having had it explained to her in the final IEP meeting in Qui's senior year of high school. She apologized and said, "In the last IEP meeting for Qui I didn't request to have the Vietnamese interpreter attend the meeting like I had done in the past. I thought the meeting was going to be simple and I would be able to understand everything. I can see now that I probably should have asked for interpreter services because I really didn't understand what this SOP is all about." The VR counselor asked whether she would like him to explain it to her more now. "Oh, yes please," replied Mrs. Tran.

The VR counselor said, "The SOP is a piece of paper that has all of the important information about Qui that people like myself need to offer continuing special services to Qui after she graduates from high school and turns 18. It has all of her records from high school, including tests she took, services she was provided, and how these services helped her succeed in high school. It also tells me things Qui wants and needs after she graduates. It gives me an idea of what to do next for Qui." He then showed Mrs. Tran the various sections of the SOP and asked her whether she understood what he was showing her and whether she had any questions. Mrs. Tran was very appreciative and said that she understood most of what he had showed her.

The VR counselor then told Mrs. Tran how he could help Qui get some job training and possibly find her a paid job in her area of interest—fashion and fashion merchandising. He said, "If Qui enjoys this work and does well at it, the next step would be for me to help her take some classes that would help her make this a career. I also would like to do some career testing with her to see other types of careers she might be interested in. Would that be okay with you?" Mrs. Tran said yes but that she was worried about Qui's safety out in the community. The VR counselor said, "I understand your

Summary of Functional Performance

Part 1: Background Information

Student name: Qui Tran   **Date of birth:** 03/24/1982   **Year of graduation/exit:** 2010

Address: 1974 Magnolia Avenue, Garden Grove, California, 92637

            (Street)   (Town, state)   (Zip code)

Telephone number: 555-867-9116   **Primary language:** Vietnamese

Current school: Garden Grove High School   **City:** Garden Grove

Student's primary disability (Diagnosis): Learning Disability

Student's secondary disability (Diagnosis), if applicable: ADHD

When was the student's disability (or disabilities) formally diagnosed? 1988; first grade

If English is not the student's primary language, what services were provided for this student as an English language learner?

ELL services provided in elementary school; ELL support provided in middle school and high school in RSP.

Date of most recent IEP or most recent 504 plan: 04/12/2010

Date this Summary was completed: 06/10/2010

This form was completed by: Name: Andrea Quan   **Title:** Transition Specialist

School: Ravenswood Unified School District   **E-mail:** aquan@rusd.k12.ca.gov

Telephone number: 555-892-3765 x27

Please check and include the most recent copy of assessment reports that you are attaching that diagnose and clearly identify the student's disability or functional limitations and/or information that will assist in postsecondary planning:

- ☒ Psychological/cognitive
- ☐ Neuropsychological
- ☒ Medical/physical
- ☒ Achievement/academics
- ☐ Adaptive behavior
- ☒ Social/interpersonal skills
- ☐ Community-based assessment
- ☒ Self-determination
- ☐ Informal assessment: _____
- ☐ Informal assessment: _____
- ☒ Other: Transition assessments: Making Action Plans: Iowa Model for Transition Assessments in Living, Learning, Working

- ☐ Response to Intervention (RTI)
- ☒ Language proficiency assessments
- ☒ Reading assessments
- ☐ Communication
- ☒ Behavioral analysis
- ☒ Classroom observations (or in other settings)
- ☒ Career/vocational or transition assessment
- ☐ Assistive technology

(continued)

Figure 3.10. Summary of Functional Performance for Qui Tran. (*Key:* ADHD, attention-deficit/hyperactivity disorder; ELL, English language learner; RSP, Resource Specialist Program; IEP, individualized education program; DSS, Disability Support Services. From Shaw, S., Kochhar-Bryant, C., Izzo, M., Benedict, K., & Parker, D. © 2005 National Transition Documentation Summit; adapted by permission.)

Figure 3.10. *(continued)*

Part 2: Student's Postsecondary Goal(s)

1. Enroll in vocational training program in fashion or fashion merchandising.
2. Obtain part-time paid employment in the fashion industry or fashion merchandising.
3. Live at home with the family and contribute to the family's income.

If employment is the primary goal, the top three job interests:

1. Clothing designer   2. Work in a fashion boutique store selling women's apparel   3. Work for a department store such as Macy's or Nordstrom selling women's apparel

Part 3: Summary of Performance (Complete all that are relevant to the student.)

ACADEMIC CONTENT AND FUNCTIONAL AREA	Present Level of Performance (grade level, standard scores, strengths, needs)	*Essential* accommodations, modifications, or assistive technology used in high school, and why needed.
Reading (Basic reading/decoding; reading comprehension; reading speed)	Woodcock-Johnson III Tests of Achievement (GL; SS): Letter–Word Identification: 10-4; 82; Reading Fluency: 8-6; 72; Story Recall: 6-3; 67; Broad Reading: 8-11; 74	Additional time for reading, shortened assignments, peer reading, use of CliffsNotes, use of CD-ROM recordings to help with reading fluency and comprehension of more technical reading materials, RSP tutorial
Math (Calculation skills, algebraic problem-solving, quantitative reasoning)	Woodcock-Johnson III Tests of Achievement (GL; SS): Calculation: 6-1; 62; Math Fluency: 8-0; 57; Applied Problems: 8-8; 71; Broad Math: 8-4; 58	Shortened assignments, calculator use, RSP tutorial
Language (written expression, speaking, spelling)	Woodcock-Johnson III Tests of Achievement (GL; SS): Writing Fluency: 10-0; 76; Writing Samples: 8-3; 63; Broad Written Language: 9-8; 78; Spelling: 10-4; 86	Extended time for assignments, RSP tutorial
Learning Skills (class participation, note taking, keyboarding, organization, homework management, time management, study skills, test-taking skills)	Good student; works hard to complete all assignments; some problems with organization skills and time management due to ADHD; study skills need further improvement; needs RSP support for taking tests, including extended time	Benefits from paraprofessional assistance in general education classrooms, will benefit from having a notetaker in college classes, will benefit from DSS services if available to help with taking tests
Career-Vocational/ Transition/ Employment (career interests, career exploration, job training, employment experiences and supports)	Interested in fashion and fashion merchandising; does not have paid employment experience; has not completed career exploration activities; would benefit from time-limited job development and supports	None offered in high school, no paid employment experience

(continued)

Figure 3.10. *(continued)*

ACADEMIC CONTENT AND FUNCTIONAL AREA	**Present Level of Performance** (grade level, standard scores, strengths, needs)	*Essential* **accommodations, modifications, or assistive technology used in high school, and why needed.**
Social Skills and Behavior (interactions with teachers/peers, level of initiation in asking for assistance, responsiveness to services and accommodations, degree of involvement in extracurricular activities, condidence and persistence as a learner)	Is generally shy and quiet. Good social skills in one-to-one interactions with trusted individuals. Compliant with teachers and authority figures; motivated to please other individuals in social interactions. Not actively involved in extracurricular activities; tends to stay at home versus socialize with peers in outside activities; very persistent learner and willing to work hard to accomplish assignments and tasks.	Participated in "Best Buddies" program in high school. Needs encouragement to get involved in social activities

Part 4: Recommendations to assist the student in meeting postsecondary goals

Suggestions for accommodations, adaptive devices, assistive services, compensatory strategies, and/or collateral support services, to enhance access in the following post-high school environments (only complete those relevant to the student's postsecondary goals).

Higher education or career-technical education	It is recommended that Qui connect with vocational education service provider for career assessment, prevocational skills training, job training, job development, and time-limited job supports. Also recommend possible community college enrollment to take some elective classes. Seek DSS assistance.
Employment	Paid employment in fashion or fashion merchandising with time-limited job supports would be beneficial.
Independent living	Qui will live at home with her family; her family is not interested in Qui living independently at the present time.
Community participation	Qui would benefit from community activities that are of interest to her; these should be explored with her, leading to her eventual participation in an activity she likes.

(continued)

Figure 3.10. *(continued)*

Part 5: Student Input (Highly Recommended)

SUMMARY OF PERFORMANCE: STUDENT PERSPECTIVE

A. How does your disability affect your schoolwork and school activities (such as grades, relationships, assignments, projects, communication, time on tests, mobility, extracurricular activities)? *My disability makes it hard for me to complete assignments on time. I need help getting started and knowing what to do. I am willing to work hard and try my best to get good grades. It is hard for me to talk to others about myself and ask for help. But I know I need the help and like working with my teachers. They have helped me a lot. I'm glad I am getting my diploma but don't know what I want to do after I graduate.*

B. In the past, what supports have been tried by teachers or by you to help you succeed in school (aids, adaptive equipment, physical accommodations, other services)? *I get help on my homework assignments and sometimes get help in my classes from my teacher's aide. She helps me understand the lesson and makes sure I write down the homework assignments in my homework log. Mrs. Leonard, my RSP teacher, helps me understand the things going on in my classes. She works with me in the RSP room every day, and this helps me a lot. I also get to take some of my tests in the RSP room and get extra time. They tell me what is on the test and help me do my best.*

C. Which of these accommodations and supports has worked best for you? *Extra time on tests and getting help in the RSP room are the things that help the best.*

D. Which of these accommodations and supports have not worked? *Asking me to keep reading it over again does not help me. I need someone else to explain it to me sometimes.*

E. What strengths and needs should professionals know you have as you enter the postsecondary education or work environment? *I am a hard worker. I want to do well in my classes and prove that I can do it. I want to get a job and make some of my own money so I can buy things for myself. I love clothes and clothes shopping. I want to get a job and do things on my own someday, but I don't know how to get started. I'm a little bit shy.*

concern, Mrs. Tran, but we provide supervision for all of our clients, and Qui's safety will be a top priority to us. We've never had a problem with any of our clients with job training or paid employment." Mrs. Tran replied, "Well, that makes me feel a bit better."

The VR counselor said the next step would be to have Qui come in by herself and begin completing the paperwork to become a client for VR services. He told Mrs. Tran that she could come with Qui to the appointment but that he wanted to work with Qui alone because she was now 18 and considered an adult. She needed to begin acting on her own behalf. However, he assured her that he would encourage Qui to share everything they do together with her. The VR counselor closed by saying, "Many Vietnamese families that I have worked with in the community have told me the importance of including the family in matters related to their children. I assure you, Mrs. Tran, I will honor and respect this with your family as well."

Mrs. Tran thanked the VR counselor for his help and said she would have Qui contact him for an appointment. "We look forward to working with you and are grateful to you for the help you can provide my daughter Qui."

SUMMARY

The roadmap to the future for a CLD youth with a disability can be found in the content of the transition IEP and SOP. These two documents, required by IDEA 2004, contain a variety of critical information and components related to the completion of high school, the transition to postsecondary settings, and a quality adult life. Transition assessment plays a key role in the development of a quality transition IEP and SOP. Along with Chapter 2, this chapter offers a number of models, methods, and questions that experts can use to gather culturally responsive transition assessment data on a CLD youth with a disability that include the perspectives of their family and friends. Special education and transition personnel can subsequently use this information to determine 1) a high school course of study; 2) transition goals, services, and supports in the areas of instruction, employment, postsecondary education, vocational training, independent living, and community participation; and 3) a relevant SOP for the CLD youth with a disability upon graduation from or completion of high school. This chapter presents sample formats for transition IEPs and SOPs along with examples of these completed documents for CLD youth with disabilities described in the case studies. The purpose of this was to provide an example of what these documents look like and how to complete them in accordance with IDEA 2004 transition services language requirements. The Pathways to Successful Transition Model, by Kochhar-Bryant and Greene (2009), offers specific language to be included in a transition IEP that corresponds with IDEA 2004 requirements. Remember that there is no required format for a transition IEP or SOP, but there *are* specific requirements for the content and language that must appear in them. Blank copies of the transition IEP and SOP used in this chapter can be found in the chapter appendix; special education and transition personnel can use these sample documents to write transition IEPs and SOPs with the knowledge that the documents will comply with federal requirements. These forms may look different from what is used in your state or district, but these are some examples of forms that comply with federal requirements.

The chapter that follows focuses on transition leadership and how special education and transition personnel can provide quality information, training, and organization change in school districts or agencies that serve CLD families, youth, and adults with disabilities.

Summary of Functional Performance

Instructions

Purpose: The Summary of Functional Performance (SOP) is required under the reauthorization of the Individuals with Disabilities Education Act of 2004 (PL 108-446), which states the following:

For a child whose eligibility under special education terminates due to graduation with a standard diploma, or due to exceeding the age of eligibility, the local education agency "shall provide the child with a summary of the child's academic achievement and functional performance, which shall include recommendations on how to assist the child in meeting the child's postsecondary goals." §300.305(e)(3)

The SOP and its accompanying documentation is important in assisting the student in the transition from high school to higher education, training, and/or employment. This information is necessary under Section 504 of the Rehabilitation Act of 1973 (PL 93-112) and the Americans with Disabilities Act of 1990 (PL 101-336) to help establish a student's eligibility for reasonable accommodations and supports in *postsecondary* settings. It is also useful for the Vocational Rehabilitation Comprehensive Assessment process. The information about a student's current level of functioning is intended to help postsecondary institutions consider accommodations for access. *These recommendations should **not** imply that any individual who qualified for special education in high school will automatically qualify for services in the postsecondary education or employment setting. Postsecondary settings will continue to make eligibility decisions on a case-by-case basis.*

The SOP is most useful when it is linked with the IEP process and when the student has the opportunity to actively participate in its development.

The SOP *must* be completed during the final year of a student's high school education. The timing of completion of the SOP may vary depending on the student's postsecondary goals. If a student is transitioning to higher education, the SOP, with additional documentation, may be necessary as the student applies to a college or university. Likewise, this information may be necessary if a student applies for services from state agencies such as VR. In some instances, it may be most appropriate to wait until the spring of a student's final year to provide an agency or employer with the most updated information on the performance of the student.

Part 1: Background Information. Complete this section as specified. Please note that this section also requests that you attach copies of the *most recent* formal and informal assessment reports that document the student's disability or functional limitations and that provide information that will assist in post–high school planning.

(continued)

From Shaw, S., Kochhar-Bryant, C., Izzo, M., Benedict, K., & Parker, D. © 2005 National Transition Documentation Summit; adapted by permission. In *Transition Planning for Culturally and Linguistically Diverse Youth* by Gary Greene (2011, Paul H. Brookes Publishing Co.)

(continued)

Part 2: Student's Postsecondary Goals. These goals should indicate the post-school environment(s) to which the student intends to participate upon completion of high school.

Part 3: Summary of Performance. This section includes three critical areas: academic, cognitive, and functional performance. For each area, please complete the student's present level of performance and the accommodations, modifications, and assistive technology that were *essential* in high school to assist the student in achieving progress. Please leave blank any section that is not applicable.

An *accommodation* is defined as a support or service that is provided to help a student fully access the general education curriculum or subject matter. Students with impaired spelling or handwriting skills, for example, may be accommodated by a notetaker or may receive permission to take class notes on a laptop computer. An accommodation *does not change the content* of what is being taught or the expectation that the student meet a performance standard applied for all students. A *modification* is defined as a change to the general education curriculum or other material being taught that alters the standards or expectations for students with disabilities. Instruction can be modified so that the material is presented differently and/or the expectations of what the student will master are changed. Modifications are not allowed in most postsecondary education environments. *Assistive technology* is defined as any device that helps a student with a disability function in a given environment; it is not limited to expensive or high-tech options. Assistive technology can include simple devices such as laminated pictures for communication, removable highlighter tapes, Velcro, and other low-tech devices.

The completion of this section may require input from a number of school personnel, including the special education teacher, the general education teacher, the school psychologist, or related services personnel. It is recommended, however, that one individual from the IEP team be responsible for gathering and organizing the information required for the SOP.

Part 4: Recommendations to Assist the Student in Meeting Postsecondary Goals. This section should present suggestions for accommodations, adaptive devices, assistive services, compensatory strategies, and/or collateral support services to enhance access in a post–high school environment, including higher education, training, employment, independent living, and/or community participation.

Part 5: Student Input. It is highly recommended that this section be completed and that the student provide information related to this SOP. The student's contribution can help 1) secondary professionals complete the summary, 2) the student better understand the impact of the disability on his or her academic and functional performance in the postsecondary setting, 3) postsecondary personnel more clearly understand the student's strengths and the impact of the disability on this student. This section may be filled out independently by the student or completed with the student through an interview.

This template was developed by the National Transition Documentation Summit © 2005 based on the initial work of Stan Shaw, Carol Kochhar-Bryant, Margo Izzo, Ken Benedict, and David Parker. It reflects the contributions and suggestions of numerous stakeholders in professional organizations, school districts, and universities. The model template was developed with the participation of the Council for Exceptional Children as well as several of its divisions, including the Division on Career Development and Transition and the Division on Learning Disabilities, and the Council on Educational Diagnostic Services, Learning Disabilities Association of America, the Higher Education Consortium for Special Education, and the Council for Learning Disabilities. *It is available to be freely copied or adapted for educational purposes.*

(continued)

Summary of Functional Performance Model Template

Part 1: Background Information

Student name: _____ Date of birth: _____ Year of graduation/exit: ____

Address: _____

(Street)   (Town, state)   (Zip code)

Telephone number: _____ Primary language: _____

Current school: _____ City: _____

Student's primary disability (Diagnosis): _____

Student's secondary disability (Diagnosis), if applicable: _____

When was the student's disability (or disabilities) formally diagnosed? _____

If English is not the student's primary language, what services were provided for this student as an English language learner?

_____

Date of most recent IEP or most recent 504 plan: _____

Date this Summary was completed: _____

This form was completed by: Name: _____ Title: _____

School: _____ E-mail: _____

Telephone number: _____

Please check and include the most recent copy of assessment reports that you are attaching that diagnose and clearly identify the student's disability or functional limitations and/or information that will assist in postsecondary planning:

- ☐ Psychological/cognitive
- ☐ Neuropsychological
- ☐ Medical/physical
- ☐ Achievement/academics
- ☐ Adaptive behavior
- ☐ Social/interpersonal skills
- ☐ Community-based assessment
- ☐ Self-determination
- ☐ Response to Intervention (RTI)
- ☐ Language proficiency assessments
- ☐ Reading assessments
- ☐ Communication
- ☐ Behavioral analysis
- ☐ Classroom observations (or in other settings)
- ☐ Career/vocational or transition assessment
- ☐ Assistive technology
- ☐ Informal assessment: _____
- ☐ Informal assessment: _____
- ☐ Other: _____

(continued)

From Shaw, S., Kochhar-Bryant, C., Izzo, M., Benedict, K., & Parker, D. © 2005 National Transition Documentation Summit; adapted by permission. In *Transition Planning for Culturally and Linguistically Diverse Youth* by Gary Greene (2011, Paul H. Brookes Publishing Co.)

(continued)

Part 2: Student's Postsecondary Goal(s)

1.
2.
3.

If employment is the primary goal, the top three job interests:

1. _____ 2. _____ 3. _____

Part 3: Summary of Performance (Complete all that are relevant to the student.)

ACADEMIC CONTENT AREA	Present Level of Performance (grade level, standard scores, strengths, needs)	*Essential* accommodations, modifications, or assistive technology used in high school, and why needed.
Reading (Basic reading/decoding, reading comprehension, reading speed)		
Math (Calculation skills, algebraic problem-solving, quantitative reasoning)		
Language (written expression, speaking, spelling)		
Learning Skills (class participation, note taking, keyboarding, organization, homework management, time management, study skills, test-taking skills)		
COGNITIVE AREAS	Present Level of Performance (grade level, standard scores, strengths, needs)	*Essential* accommodations, modifications, or assistive technology used in high school, and why needed.
General Ability and Problem Solving (reasoning/processing)		

(continued)

GOGNITIVE AREAS *(continued)*	**Present Level of Performance** (grade level, standard scores, strengths, needs)	***Essential* accommodations, modifications, or assistive technology used in high school, and why needed.**
Attention and Executive Functioning (energy level, sustained attention, memory functions, processing speed, impulse control, activity level)		
Communication (speech/language, assisted communication)		
FUNCTIONAL AREAS	**Present Level of Performance** (strengths and needs)	***Essential* accommodations, modifications, or assistive technology used in high school, and why needed.**
Social Skills and Behavior (Interactions with teachers/peers, level of initiation in asking for assistance, responsiveness to services and accommodations, degree of involvement in extracurricular activities, confidence and persistence as a learner)		
Independent Living Skills (Self-care, leisure skills, personal safety, transportation, banking, budgeting)		

From Shaw, S., Kochhar-Bryant, C., Izzo, M., Benedict, K., & Parker, D. © 2005 National Transition Documentation Summit; adapted by permission. In *Transition Planning for Culturally and Linguistically Diverse Youth* by Gary Greene (2011, Paul H. Brookes Publishing Co.)

(continued)

FUNCTIONAL AREAS *(continued)*	Present Level of Performance (strengths and needs)	*Essential* accommodations, modifications, or assistive technology used in high school, and why needed.
Environmental Access/Mobility (assistive technology, mobility, transportation)		
Self-Determination/ Self-Advocacy Skills (Ability to identify and articulate postsecondary goals, learning strengths and needs)		
Career-Vocational/ Transition/ Employment (Career interests, career exploration, job training, employment experiences and supports)		
Additional important considerations that can assist in making decisions about disability determination and needed accommodations (e.g., medical problems, family concerns, sleep disturbance)		

From Shaw, S., Kochhar-Bryant, C., Izzo, M., Benedict, K., & Parker, D. © 2005 National Transition Documentation Summit; adapted by permission. In *Transition Planning for Culturally and Linguistically Diverse Youth* by Gary Greene (2011, Paul H. Brookes Publishing Co.)

(continued)

Part 4: Recommendations to assist the student in meeting postsecondary goals

Suggestions for accommodations, adaptive devices, assistive services, compensatory strategies, and/or collateral support services, to enhance access in the following post-high school environments (only complete those relevant to the student's postsecondary goals).

Higher education or career-technical education	
Employment	
Independent living	
Community participation	

Part 5: Student Input (Highly Recommended)

SUMMARY OF PERFORMANCE: STUDENT PERSPECTIVE

A. How does your disability affect your schoolwork and school activities (such as grades, relationships, assignments, projects, communication, time on tests, mobility, extracurricular activities)?

B. In the past, what supports have been tried by teachers or by you to help you succeed in school (aids, adaptive equipment, physical accommodations, other services)?

C. Which of these accommodations and supports has worked best for you?

D. Which of these accommodations and supports have not worked?

E. What strengths and needs should professionals know about you as you enter the postsecondary education or work environment?

I have reviewed and agree with the content of this Summary of Performance.

Student signature: _____ Date: _____

Transition Individualized Education Program

Vision	**Career interests**	**Strengths**

Present level of performance

Academics:

Community:

Employment:

Postsecondary training and learning:

Transition service needs

-
-
-
-

Needed transition services

Instruction:

Community:

Employment:

Related services:

Daily living:

Transition goals

Instruction:

Community:

Employment:

Supplementary and related services:

4

The Role of Teacher Leadership in Promoting Organizational Change and Successful Transition for Culturally and Linguistically Diverse Youth with Disabilities

Jennifer Summers is a 27-year-old White woman who teaches special education in a predominantly Latino high school in El Paso, Texas. Marion Johnson is a 30-year-old White woman who teaches special education at an inner-city high school in Baltimore, Maryland, with a large African American population. The two met recently at a national conference sponsored by the Council for Exceptional Children. They had attended a session on transition for CLD youth with disabilities and were inspired by the content of the presentation. They went to lunch together afterward and shared a variety of thoughts and reactions to the presentation.

"It's amazing how that presenter described the problems faced by Latino parents when it comes to transition planning for their kids. That's exactly what I've seen in my school district at transition IEP meetings," said Jennifer.

"I agree," replied Marion. "Many of those same issues apply to the African American parents I've worked with in secondary IEP meetings. I get the problems, but how do I get started working on solutions?"

Jennifer replied, "Well, the presenter had a lot of really good ideas, like that working in teams can really make a difference."

Marion said, "True. In my school district we're using professional learning communities. Maybe I can get one going with some of the other high school special education teachers who share my frustration with the transition planning process for our African American families."

"I hear you," replied Jennifer, "but finding the time and resources to do these things is what really makes it challenging. We're facing massive budget cuts in the next several years. I'm just hoping to keep my job!"

"I know," said Marion, "but as the presenter said, you've got to have a vision and start somewhere. The journey of a thousand miles begins with the first step."

This conversation sets the stage for the topic of this chapter: the role of teacher leadership in promoting organizational change and successful transition for CLD youth with disabilities. In my career as a special education teacher, mentor teacher, conference presenter, and college professor of special education, I have frequently advocated ideas that reflect my personal vision and passion for improving the quality of education for *all* individuals in the public schools, including CLD youth with disabilities. Occasionally these ideas are met with comments such as "You have no idea what things are like at my school. We could never do that!" I have been known to respond to this somewhat negative "can't do" statement with the following: "I'm not here to reflect reality. I'm here to create cognitive dissonance in you." This response is by no means meant to communicate disrespect, a lack of sympathy, or a lack of empathy to the person sharing his or her perspective on change. Quite the contrary, I taught special education in the public schools for 10 years and have been employed as a professor at a public university for more than 23 years; I know the challenges and difficulties faced by those of us in public education. However, supporting teachers as leaders is one of the best ways to go about promoting organizational change and improving public education. Teachers can make a difference!

The following questions guide the discussion in this chapter:

1.   What is the definition and what are the characteristics of teacher leadership?

2.   How can teacher leadership be promoted in the public schools?

3.   What strategies can be used by teacher leaders to promote organizational change in their schools or districts?

Answers to these important questions come from a variety of sources. This chapter presents published literature on teacher leadership, interviews with leaders in the field of education, organizational change strategies, and case studies illustrating ways to promote teacher leadership and organizational change. The chapter begins with an exploration of the definition and characteristics of teacher leadership.

WHAT IS THE DEFINITION AND WHAT ARE THE CHARACTERISTICS OF TEACHER LEADERSHIP?

A search of the literature revealed the lack of a consistent definition or operationalization of the term *teacher leadership*. Rather, the *characteristics of teacher leadership* are more commonly presented in articles on this topic. Table 4.1 lists many of the characteristics of teacher leaders described in the literature. Terms such as *visionary, change agent, problem solver, motivator, influencer, organizer, coach,* and *mentor* are commonly used to describe teacher leaders.

> There is a lack of a consistent definition of the term teacher leadership in published literature on the topic.

Pounder (2006) reviewed the literature on the topic of teacher leadership. He cited the work of Silva, Gimbert, and Nolan (2000), who argued that three stages or waves of the study of teacher leadership have developed over time. The first wave viewed teacher leadership from an organizational hierarchy perspective, as exemplified by the department head within a school. The second wave focused more on the instructional aspects and function of teaching but still conceptualized teacher leaders as being in organizational positions of authority, such as team leader or curriculum developer. The third wave, which represents the current view of teacher leadership, sees teaching and leadership as integrated notions: Teachers demonstrate their leadership skills in

Table 4.1. Characteristics associated with teacher leadership

Visionary	Knowledgeable	Highly skilled	Trustworthy	Transformational
Passionate	Credible	Professional	Collegial	Effective
Engaging	Inspirational	Encouraging	Change agent	Responsible
Highly esteemed	Mentor	Reflective	Influential	
Problem solver	Role model	Builder	Cultivating	
Ethical	Decisive	Focused	Intelligent	
Communicative	Organizer	Perceptive	Involved	
Focused	Global thinker	Supportive	Accepting	
Resourceful	Driven	Risk taker	Process oriented	
Managerial	Charismatic	Motivational	Active	
Nurturing	Value driven	Socially conscious	Guider	
Listener	Facilitator	and politically involved	Accountable	
Excellent	Empowered	Growth oriented		
Authoritative	Powerful	Open		

the process of their day-to-day functioning within their classrooms and schools. "This conceptualization of teacher leadership is grounded on professionalism and collegiality and is a label reserved for teachers who improve a school's educational climate and by engaging colleagues in various activities designed to enhance the education process" (Pounder, 2006, p. 534). Pounder also cited the work of Lieberman, Saxl, and Miles (1988), who identified 18 skills characterizing teacher leaders, which they classified as follows:

1. Building trust and rapport
2. Engaging in organizational diagnosis
3. Dealing with the process
4. Using resources
5. Managing the work
6. Building skill and confidence in others

Finally, Crowther (1997) conducted a study of teacher leadership in a socially disadvantaged setting that mirrored the challenges faced by special education and transition personnel engaged in the transition planning process with low-SES CLD families of youth with disabilities. Crowther described teacher leaders as "individuals acclaimed not only for their pedagogical excellence, but also for their influence in stimulating change and creating improvement in the schools and socioeconomically disadvantaged communities in which they work" (p. 6). The criteria for Crowther's selection of teacher leaders in his study included the following:

1. Displayed concrete evidence of a significant contribution to an aspect of social justice in the school or school community
2. Highly esteemed in the community, particularly among socioeconomically disadvantaged individuals and groups
3. Recognized by colleagues as very influential in school decision-making processes
4. Accorded a high level of school-based responsibility by colleagues and the school administration (Pounder, 2006, p. 535)

These types of qualities are what Bass (1985) described as examples of *transformational leadership,* arguing that effective leaders are individuals who display behaviors that are more active than passive in nature. According to Bass, characteristics associated with transformational leadership include

1. Idealized influence or charisma
2. Inspirational motivation
3. Individual consideration
4. Intellectual stimulation

Transformational teacher leaders are individuals who have a deep commitment to a set of core values and are able to communicate these values in enthusiastic ways that resonate with others, inspire them, and raise their expectations. Moreover, transformational leaders are individuals who 1) encourage change; 2) challenge the status quo; 3) demonstrate openness to new ways of doing things; and 4) can successfully model, mentor, and coach others in the change process (Darling-Hammond & McLaughlin, 1995; Silva et al., 2000).

> Transformational teacher leaders are individuals who have a deep commitment to a set of core values and are able to communicate these in enthusiastic ways that resonate with and inspire other teachers.

In summary, the literature on teacher leadership presents ample indicators of how teacher leaders act and behave rather than a concise definition of what teacher leaders are. The previous chapters discussed in depth the problems faced by CLD families and youth with disabilities in the transition planning process and the need for more culturally responsive, knowledgeable, and skilled special education and transition personnel. Teacher leadership can play an important role in the transformation of these problems and challenges. I next discuss how to promote this type of leadership in teachers who are involved in transition planning with CLD families and youth with disabilities.

HOW CAN TEACHER LEADERSHIP BE PROMOTED IN THE PUBLIC SCHOOLS?

Vehicles for the promotion of teacher leadership in the public schools come both from within the system and from outside of the system. Examples of ways to promote teacher leadership within the public schools include

1. Teacher empowerment
2. Professional development
3. Use of professional learning communities (PLCs)
4. Use of action research

Continuing higher education is the most typical outside-the-system vehicle for promoting teacher leadership in public education. A review of both systems of teacher leadership development follows.

Teacher Empowerment

Employees within an organization are empowered when they are given the power to experience a sense of ownership and control of their jobs, their working conditions, and the direction of the organization. This definition of empowerment is rooted in the corporate world, but its counterpart in education is teacher empowerment (Terry, 2007). Bolin (1989) defined *teacher empowerment* as investing teachers with the right to participate in the determination of school goals and policies and to exercise professional judgment about what and how to teach. Others have defined *teacher empowerment* as being a function of 1) school administrators being ready and willing to share autonomy with others whose commitment is necessary to make the educational program function to a maximum degree of efficiency, 2) the development of a school environment in which teachers act and are treated as professionals, and 3) teachers being provided with a sense of ownership in the mission of the school and a vital interest in the school's effectiveness (Lee, 1991; Lucas, Brown, and Marcus, 1991). Terry added that teacher empowerment shifts the focus of control for the substance of the school organization from the principal to teachers. It is an evolutionary process that is dependent upon principals who trust their teachers and teachers who trust their principal. Trust, in turn, allows teachers to feel free to be creative and take risks to grow and improve their professional knowledge and skills.

> *Teacher empowerment invests teachers with the right to participate in determining school goals and policies and to exercise professional judgment about what and how to teach (Bolin, 1989).*

Schools can empower teachers by providing them with a supportive environment that encourages them to examine and reflect upon their teaching and school practice. There are several ways to do this. First, principals can "ask more than tell" (Reitzug, 1991). For example, principals could spend more time asking their special education and transition personnel how they think the transition IEP process could be improved to be more culturally responsive rather than telling them how this can be accomplished. "The principal's role shifts from prescribing substance to facilitating methods in which substance can be discovered" (Terry, 2007, p. 6). This does not mean that principals cannot play an active role in the process by suggesting a variety of alternatives for teachers to consider. However, Lucas et al. (1991) stated that 1) the more power is given away, the more powerful all leaders become; and 2) principals who create teacher leaders are ultimately more powerful than those who do not.

Second, the school can create democratic learning communities. Williams, Cate, and O'Hair (2009) presented a comprehensive review of this literature on school leadership and noted that traditional school structures today can be characterized as bureaucracies dominated by top-down leadership that isolates teachers, creates a culture that affects educational quality in a negative way, and discourages systematic school change. Principals can facilitate the creation of a democratic learning community by establishing mechanisms through which they can obtain regular input from staff; provide staff with meaningful leadership roles; and allow staff to assume roles that promote learning, reflection, and action that leads to change (Morrisey, Cowan, Leo, & Blair, 1999). "Leadership in a democratic school is viewed as being embodied in acts that may come from anyone in the school community, including teachers, students, and parents" (Reitzug & O'Hair, 2002, p. 122). Hence, this strategy for empowerment goes beyond the democratic involvement of teachers alone and expands the notion to the entire school community. This strategy speaks to the recommendations of

Darling-Hammond (1997), who argued that establishing a democratic community requires intensive knowledge on the part of all actors in the system. Likewise, Murphy (2002) stated that social justice, school improvement, and the creation of democratic learning communities is accomplished best when a school leader focuses efforts on involving multiple stakeholders in a school community by nurturing and increasing their meaningful involvement in the school decision-making process.

Principals can facilitate the creation of a democratic learning community by establishing mechanisms through which they can obtain regular input from staff; provide staff with meaningful leadership roles; and allow staff to assume roles that promote learning, reflection, and action that leads to change (Morrisey et al., 1999).

How would this apply to the example of making the transition IEP process more culturally responsive for CLD families and youth with disabilities? A democratic school principal not only would ask special education and transition personnel for their input on how to accomplish this task but would also seek input from CLD youth with disabilities, their families, and the greater CLD school community. In this way, "schools move toward democracy by encouraging 'participation, communication, and cross-cultural cooperation'" (Furman & Shields, 2003, p. 8).

Third, teachers can be encouraged to engage in reflective practice (Terry, 2007). Data-based decision making and action research are two highly recommended strategies for doing this. Both involve teachers asking questions about their pedagogy, exploring and implementing new techniques to improve their skills, and gathering data to determine the success of their efforts. (Action research is discussed more later in this chapter.) Terry argued that principals who encourage and facilitate engagement in reflective practices enable teachers to study their teaching in a proactive manner.

Finally, schools can create a supportive environment for promoting teacher empowerment by providing sufficient resources (e.g., money, materials, time, opportunity; Terry, 2007). Teachers must receive essential incentives and supports such as these when being encouraged to grow and change. Other options should be explored and discussed when teacher requests for resources cannot be fulfilled (i.e., in times of budget cuts and restrictions). These options include grants, local business partnerships, and state or federal incentives (Terry, 2007). "Principals must view teachers in the leadership capacity role as being capable of making pertinent contacts outside of the school other than with only parents" (p. 6).

The following case study illustrates the provision of a supportive environment for promoting special education teacher empowerment in the transition of CLD youth with disabilities.

Alvarado High School Transition Services

Jaime Gutierrez is in his second year of teaching special education at Alvarado High School in Mesa, Arizona. He is enrolled in a master's in special education degree program at a local university and is taking a course on transition and career development for youth with disabilities. Part of the course has focused on transition services for CLD youth with disabilities as well as teacher leadership and empowerment. Jaime expressed to his professor that he is frustrated with the transition process in place at Alvarado High School. In particular, Jaime is concerned with the lack of knowledge and skills of a number of his colleagues for how to engage in culturally responsive transition planning with Latino families that speak limited English. He feels that too often the transition IEP team does not make meaningful connections with CLD families of youth with disabilities, resulting in the team's lack of understanding of the family's unique circumstances and cultural viewpoints on transition and the future of their child. Jaime speaks Spanish, has a similar background to many of the families on his caseload, and has been studying in his graduate program the things he feels are needed to improve transition services at Alvarado High School. The challenge for Jaime is that he is the newest special education teacher on the staff, and most of his colleagues have been teaching at the school for a long time. Jaime feels that he has something to offer the staff to improve the quality of transition services for CLD families of youth with disabilities. His professor has encouraged him to talk to his principal and explore some of the teacher empowerment and leadership strategies discussed in the course he is taking.

The principal had an initial meeting with Jaime, provided Jaime ample opportunity to discuss his concerns, and spent the majority of the time listening rather than talking. The principal scheduled a follow-up meeting with Jaime for the near future and asked Jaime to gather some data to support his claims and concerns in the interim.

"I can see, Jaime, that you've done your homework," said the principal shortly after reviewing the data with Jaime at the next meeting. "I share your concern that the special education team as a whole may not be as capable as you in terms of working with CLD families to create culturally responsive transition IEPs. So what do you think we should do, and how can I help you do this?" Jaime replied, "Well, I don't think it's a good idea to go after the entire special education staff at Alvarado at this point because I don't want to make any enemies." The principal replied, "That's probably wise, but nevertheless, we've got a problem here and as the leader of this school, I can't allow it to continue indefinitely. What might be a first step, Jaime? Any suggestions?" Jaime replied, "Our district and you in particular have been encouraging teachers to engage in action research. I would love to spend some time talking with some of our CLD parents about their experiences with the transition IEP process, maybe look into some things other school districts with similar demographics to ours are doing, and maybe try out a few of these ideas with some of the CLD families that have upcoming transition IEP meetings later on this year." "I think that would great, Jaime. I'd like to support you as best I can in the process. What resources do you think you would need to do this?"

Jaime said, "Not many. A lot of these things I can do during my prep time. I have to take an action research class in my graduate program, so let me talk to my advisor and see if I can use this as my project and maybe get started on it early. The best time to talk to families is after school hours and during the evenings at their homes or someplace in the community, like at their church."

The principal replied, "Well, I've got a small pot of money in my principal's discretionary fund that I was given by our community parent support organization. I'm willing to offer you a small stipend, say $300 to $500, for the after-school meetings you would have with the families, depending on how much time you have to put in."

Jaime said, "Thank you; that's a very generous offer. Let me get back to you with a proposal of the families I want to meet with and how much time I think it will take, and we'll go from there."

"Great," said the principal, "It's nice to work with an enthusiastic teacher like you who is interested in making things better for our school and community. I look forward to supporting you in this project!"

The case study of Jaime Gutierrez highlights many of the characteristics of teacher empowerment and strategies for promoting teacher leadership discussed thus far. It is clear that Jaime was interested in making a significant contribution to an aspect of social justice in his school and school community (Crowther, 1997); specifically, he wanted to improve the quality of transition planning for Latino families of youth with disabilities that speak limited English. He believed that they were disenfranchised by the current process because the transition IEP team was unable to make meaningful connections with them. It is also evident that Jaime possessed a number of the qualities of transformational leadership described by Bass (1985), such as inspirational motivation and intellectual stimulation. Jaime was enrolled in a master's degree program in special education, had been inspired by what he was learning in his coursework, and had spoken to one of his professors about things that he was learning in class and wanted to put into practice in his school.

The case study also contains evidence of the school principal promoting teacher leadership and empowerment. The principal's interactions with Jaime demonstrate the ask-more-than-tell leadership recommendation of Reitzug (1991). The principal never told Jaime how to solve the problem but instead asked questions that encouraged Jaime to explore his own ways of improving the quality of transition planning for CLD families of youth with disabilities at Alvarado High School. Power was given away (Lucas et al., 1991) by the school principal to Jaime as a result of this approach. Moreover, the principal offered Jaime a meaningful leadership role by accepting his proposal to gain input from past CLD parents who had completed the transition planning process and to contact other school districts to learn about culturally responsive transition IEP practices. The principal also accepted and encouraged Jaime's idea to engage in action research, which would allow Jaime the opportunity to assume a leadership role that promotes learning, reflection, and action to solve problems (Morrisey et al., 1999). Finally, the principal showed evidence of creating a supportive environment for teacher leadership and empowerment by offering Jaime a stipend for taking extra time and effort outside of the regular school day to meet and collaborate with CLD families of youth with disabilities to find out their perspectives of the transition IEP process at Alvarado High School.

Professional Development

Professional development, also known as *staff development,* is a long-standing within-system practice for advancing teacher knowledge and skill. It is designed to promote teacher empowerment and school system change. However, because of the way it has historically been implemented in public education, it has often failed to achieve its intended outcomes. School professional development has been implemented in response to federal, state, or local school district mandates and external initiatives as opposed to teacher-determined, teacher-desired areas of professional growth. In addition, resources for implementing follow-up training and support for teachers to implement professional growth initiatives in their classrooms are often sorely lacking. This can result in what some have referred to as the "train and pray" or the "greenhouse effect" of professional development. The latter likens teachers who receive professional development to plants or flowers that grow in a greenhouse. They bloom early, but their petals and leaves die quickly when removed from the greenhouse if not given sustaining nutrients and care to help them continue to grow.

Individuals conducting professional development can do a number of key things to maximize the effectiveness of professional development:

Much of school professional development occurs in response to federal, state, or local school district mandates or external initiatives as opposed to teacher-determined, teacher-desired areas of professional growth.

1. Use interviews or presession surveys to gain input from administrators and training participants regarding their knowledge, skills, and needs on the topic to be presented.

2. Design the training to meet the unique needs of the audience based on their input.

3. Share the training objectives, agenda, or outline, and provide multiple opportunities for participants to engage in guided practice, perform application activities, ask questions, and discuss the material.

4. Conduct the training in a comfortable setting and attend to participants' creature comforts (i.e., provide food and drink, breaks, lunch).

5. Incorporate the use of technology (i.e., laptop computer, projector, PowerPoint slides, streamed video) wisely and in ways that enhance the training rather than distract participants from learning the critical content.

6. Make sure all technology has been pretested and is ready to go before beginning the presentation.

7. Provide handouts in the form of either guided notes or copies of the PowerPoint slides with adequate room for participants to take notes.

8. Present the material in an engaging, enthusiastic manner and in a way that captures and maintains the participants' attention.

9. Check frequently to determine the degree to which participants are processing and comprehending the material being presented.

10. Actively model the knowledge and skills participants are to develop.

11. Summarize periodically the main points of the presentation and build in smooth transitions between key content.

12. Conduct a knowledge and skills posttest at the end of the training and compare the results to participants' presession survey results.

13. Provide an opportunity for participants to evaluate the quality of the content, materials, and activities at the end of the training as well as to identify follow-up activities and support that they feel they need in order to effectively apply the training in their classrooms or schools.

Interview with Dr. Bill Beacham: The Essential Components of Quality Professional Development and Training

Dr. Bill Beacham was trained as a school counselor and holds a bachelor's degree in psychology, a master's degree in pupil personnel services and school psychology, and a doctorate in clinical psychology with a specialty in addictive disorders. Dr. Beacham has more than 30 years of experience in the public schools, having worked as a high school counselor and in professional staff development. He has provided training for the U.S. Olympic Committee, various police departments across the nation, and countless school districts.

What do you feel is the best way to provide professional development and leadership training to teachers who are working in CLD communities?

The training must be systematic and structured. Sometimes you rely on internal people to conduct the training, and sometimes you rely on outside experts to lead the way. You utilize leadership from the top and from the bottom, depending on the situation. For example, training should come from the top when policy development is needed and then this has to filter down to educate staff through further professional development activities. Regardless, structured levels of leadership and commitment must occur at all levels.

Professional development must utilize data and be data driven to be effective. This requires enormous amounts of collaborative input from all stakeholders in the process. When people feel included in the process and have a forum in which to express their thoughts and ideas, they feel safe. Participants need to be able to talk, to be acknowledged, and listened to in order to move forward. Right now we're in a huge change process in public education. There's a grieving process going on with teachers over what has been taken away from them. They've had to face drastic budget cuts, class size increases, furlough days, and even 4-day work weeks proposed in some school districts. Professional developers need to acknowledge the sense of grief and loss in teachers, otherwise teachers will sense denial from those of us providing professional development.

"Quality professional development should be data driven, systematic, and structured. It should include input from all stakeholders in the process" (Dr. Bill Beacham, personal communication, August 12, 2010).

Nevertheless, in this environment, we need to move forward. We need to remind teachers like we remind our students in our classrooms each week that "every Monday matters!" Every Monday, teachers have the opportunity to set the agenda for the upcoming week for their students. Likewise, professional development needs to set this agenda for teachers. We need to reignite their passion and [remind them] why they are teaching.

Quality professional development has to create a sense of shared responsibility, commitment, and passion in teachers. We as a culture don't do this well; we compete, avoid, compromise, and accommodate. Competition produces winners and losers, and we wind up with more losers. Avoiders say, "Just leave me alone." Accommodators do the minimum of what you ask them to do, not bad enough to derail the initiative, but not enough to help the initiative move forward. Sometimes they put up roadblocks. Compromisers either accept too much or too little, rather than communicating their own preferences. And then we have the BMWs—"bitchers," moaners, and whiners. You can encounter all of these types of individuals when conducting professional development, and if you don't focus in on their underlying needs, the process will not work.

So how do you do this? How do you focus in on the underlying needs of teachers in professional development?

You begin by trying to build a relationship with the teachers you are training. You need to connect with them, bond, and develop attachments between them and you. Listening to them and understanding their underlying needs is how you go about doing this. As I said earlier, you need to provide them with a forum in which they feel safe physically, psychologically, and emotionally. You acknowledge them. But at a certain point, you need to begin to move forward.

Effective professional development with teachers teaches them how to collaborate together and the essentials of good communication skills. This includes things such as eye contact between people when speaking, proper vocal tone, and setting a climate that allows others to tell their story or perspective. These attending behaviors are necessary to help people connect with one another. Collaborative groups by nature can be fraught with conflict due to differing backgrounds and needs of participants. Ground rules around collaboration need to be discussed and set. Effective trainers must coach teachers in the necessary skills for sound communication. It's more about the process than the product. What you do to facilitate the process is very important.

"Good professional development is like serving a good meal. You begin by setting the table. You serve the meal. You. . .check in with the eaters to see if they like what they have been served. . . . You may have to adjust the recipe a bit but hopefully, you will not be left with having to clean up a mess" (Dr. Bill Beacham, personal communication, August 12, 2010).

Good professional development is like preparing and serving a good meal. You begin by setting the table. You serve the meal. You constantly check in with the eaters to see if they like what they have been served. You have to be a good listener and filter things well, knowing what to respond to and what not to be concerned about and proceed accordingly. You may have to adjust the recipe a bit, but hopefully you will not be left with having to clean up a mess. Effective professional development is a comprehensive and well-researched, developed, implemented, and monitored process.

Professional Learning Communities

The concept of PLCs originated with Richard DuFour, former Superintendent of Adlai Stevenson High School in Lincolnshire, Illinois. DuFour's advocacy for PLCs occurred during the school reform and restructuring movement that took place in the 1990s. DuFour (2004) stated, "The professional learning community model is a grand design—a powerful new way of working together that profoundly affects the practices of schooling" (p. 6). The focus of a PLC is on learning rather than teaching, on working collaboratively, and on holding teachers and schools accountable for producing results. Three critical questions guide the work of teachers participating in a PLC (DuFour, 2004):

IMPLICATIONS FOR PRACTICE

PLCs focus on learning rather than teaching, on working collaboratively, and on holding teachers and schools accountable for producing results. How could you use a PLC to improve transition planning at your school?

1. What do teachers want each student to learn?
2. How will they know when each student has learned it?
3. How will they respond when a student experiences difficulty learning?

A key component of PLCs associated with teacher empowerment and teacher leadership is collaboration. Establishing a culture of collaboration is essential for educators who wish to build a successful PLC (DuFour, 2004). Teachers must work together to achieve the collective purpose of learning for all students. Teachers can collaborate best for school improvement by working in teams, engaging in ongoing questioning and analysis that promote deep team learning and improvement in classroom practice. Teams should 1) develop common formative assessments that are authentic and valid for determining student mastery of learning; 2) decide when to administer these assessments; and 3) continually engage in collaborative conversations that analyze the results, generating strategies and products focused on improving results. DuFour argued that "this focus on continual improvement and results requires educators to change traditional practices and revise prevalent assumptions" and "educators who focus on results must also stop limiting improvement goals to factors outside the classroom" (p. 6).

The philosophy and implementation of PLCs supports the notion of teacher empowerment, shared leadership, and collective values and visions. A common PLC implementation approach principals use is to create school-based grade-level teams of teachers who meet periodically throughout the year. This requires principals to provide teachers with common planning time. Another less-structured approach to developing effective PLCs is through allowing teachers to develop their own grass roots efforts to inquire about particular teaching practices (Jacobson, 2010). Yet the strength of this approach is also its weakness. It allows for more teacher self-direction but does not provide enough administrative oversight and direction for the teams and may underestimate the value of monitoring ongoing assessment results. However, Jacobson pointed out that a results-oriented, top-down approach to PLCs (i.e., teacher leadership teams created by the school principal) can sometimes lead to superficial implementation, a focus on short-term results, and a limited capacity for teachers to engage in deep-level analysis.

Regardless of which approach is used, PLCs represent a viable teacher empowerment and teacher leadership strategy. This begs the question of how PLCs can work to promote culturally responsive transition planning for CLD families and youth with disabilities. The answer lies in the creation of PLCs whose purpose is to question, explore, gather data, and create processes and products that demonstrate effective CLD transition planning practices in a school or school district. A suggested set of steps that schools can do to accomplish this would be to

1. Identify potential members for the PLC team (e.g., general education, special education, transition services teachers), which should also include students, CLD families of youth with disabilities, and respected members of the CLD community

2. Generate key questions regarding culturally responsive transition planning with CLD families of youth with disabilities (e.g., What is the present level of knowledge and skills of school staff in this area? What are the current transition planning practices used at this school? What things need to occur to improve the quality of collaboration between school staff and families during the transition planning process?)

3. Develop authentic and valid formative assessments that will provide data regarding the quality of CLD transition planning practices and areas in which improvement is needed (e.g., conduct qualitative interviews with current and former families regarding the degree of culturally responsive collaboration used in the transition planning process; develop satisfaction surveys for families to complete after participating in a transition planning meeting; gather follow-up data on the quality of adult life of CLD youth with disabilities who have graduated or completed high school)

4. Designate potential strategies for program improvement if data indicate that CLD transition planning practices are unsatisfactory (e.g., form a subcommittee to study and develop program improvement efforts and then to report back to the larger PLC)

O'Hair, McLaughlin, and Reitzug (2000) proposed the IDEALS framework for creating and maintaining democratic learning communities: Inquiry, Discourse, Equity, Authenticity, Leadership, and Service. This model "includes inquiring about practices, supporting discourse about learning, focusing on equity issues, making learning connections with the real world, sharing leadership, and promoting service" (Williams et al., 2009, p. 456). These are the essential components of quality PLCs. DuFour added that initiating and sustaining the PLC concept requires hard work, collaboration, accountability, and a focus on results and continual improvement:

> The rise or fall of the professional learning community concept depends not on the merits of the concept itself, but on the most important element in the improvement of any school–the commitment and persistence of the educators within it. (2004, p. 6)

Action Research

Action research is another strategy for promoting teacher leadership in the public schools. Since 1997, it has drawn the attention of teachers, administrators, and policy makers in the United States (Mills, 2007). Action research offers an outstanding opportunity for teachers to investigate and obtain data about their students, teaching, classrooms, or schools. They can then use this information to evaluate the quality of their educational practices, allowing them to exercise leadership skills designed for educational improvement.

Mills (2007) defined action research as

> Any systematic inquiry conducted by teachers, administrators, counselors, or others with a vested interest in the teaching and learning process or environment for the purpose of gathering information about how their particular schools operate, how they teach, and how their students learn.

Action research is done *by teachers* and is *for teachers*. The focus is on teachers' own classrooms, and the process often involves systematic inquiry into their own instructional methods, students, and assessments. The goal of action research is for teachers to better understand these aspects of their teaching in order to improve their effectiveness as instructors (Mertler, 2009).

The basic process of conducting action research involves four steps:

Action research is done by teachers *and is* for teachers. *Its purpose is for teachers to gather information about how their schools operate, how they teach, and how their students learn.*

1. Identifying an area of focus
2. Collecting data
3. Analyzing and interpreting the data
4. Developing a plan of action (Mills, 2007)

The process does not require formal education and training in research methodology as is typically the case in scientific research. However, the guiding principles are the same because 1) questions or problems are posed for investigation; 2) potential solutions are generated; 3) action is taken on the solution that seems best able to solve the problem; 4) data are gathered and analyzed to determine whether the action taken was effective; and 5) the action or solution is evaluated and revised if necessary, allowing for further action research to take place in order to maximize the effectiveness of the solution.

The case study of Jaime Gutierrez, the special education teacher at Alvarado High School, presents an example of action research. Jaime expressed concern to his school principal that his special education colleagues were not engaging in culturally responsive collaboration with CLD families of youth with disabilities during the transition planning process. He was concerned that this was resulting in a lack of quality connection with these families during transition IEP meetings and the creation of lower quality transition IEPs for CLD youth with disabilities at Alvarado High School. His principal asked Jaime to propose a potential solution to this problem. Jaime responded that he would like to engage in action research; his school district and principal were encouraging teachers to do this, and Jaime was going to take an action research class in his graduate program. Jaime's action research proposal involved him 1) interviewing CLD parents of youth with disabilities to share their experiences with the transition IEP process, 2) looking into things that other school districts in the area with similar demographics were doing with CLD families in the transition planning process, and 3) applying what he learned to CLD families that had transition IEP meetings scheduled in the coming year. A fourth critical step that Jaime should do in his action research project is to evaluate the effectiveness of his collaboration with CLD families during the transition IEP process and the specific outcomes that occurred as a result of this collaboration. He should then engage in further actions to refine the solutions and gather data on their effectiveness. Thus, action research is an ongoing, cyclical process.

Mertler (2009) presented an extensive list of what action research is and is not. According to him, action research is

1. A process that improves education, in general by incorporating change
2. A process of educators working together to improve their own practice
3. Collaborative and composed of educators talking and working together in empowering relationships
4. Practical and relevant to teachers, allowing for critical reflection to occur
5. Planned, systematic, open-minded, requiring teachers to "test" ideas about education
6. A justification of one's own educational practices (pp. 18–19)

Mertler (2009) stated that action research is not a fad that involves the simple implementation of a predetermined, externally imposed solution to a problem. Action research is more than problem solving; it involves specifying a problem, developing something new and different (in most cases), and reflecting critically on its effectiveness. Moreover, action research often is not conclusively right or wrong; rather, it leads to tentative solutions based on observations and other data collection that require ongoing monitoring, evaluation, and refinement. Perhaps most important is that action research "is *not* done 'to' or 'by' other people; it is research that is done by particular educators, on their own work, with students and colleagues" (p. 19).

In summary, action research is clearly associated with the notion of teacher leadership and empowerment because it encourages teachers to take risks to make change, act as their own decision makers, and creatively design and propose unique solutions to everyday problems they encounter in their practice. It allows them to use their own expertise, talents, and abilities to exert leadership in producing school improvement. "This approach to school leadership and improvement is in complete opposition to the standard top-down, administrator-driven leadership" in the public schools (Mertler, 2009, p. 21). "The locus of control is in essence returned to the classroom level, thereby enhancing the effectiveness of schools and promoting school improvement" (Johnson, as cited in Mertler, 2009, p. 21).

To carry this one step further, might not action research be used with the student as the change agent? As the locus of control moves to teacher leadership, so, too, might the student be a partner in this leadership. Chapter 2 presented strong arguments for student involvement in transition IEPs. The students know their culture and family best; their empowerment to lead and guide the transition planning process is key to improved postschool outcomes.

Continuing Higher Education

As stated earlier, continuing higher education has historically been the most typical outside-the-system vehicle for promoting teacher leadership and advancement. Most school districts offer advancement on the salary schedule for teachers who complete additional graduate units after their initial hiring. These are known as continuing education units (CEUs). Attending professional development conferences, seminars, or trainings that offer CEUs is another option for teacher advancement besides taking graduate coursework at a college or university.

Most school districts offer advancement on the salary schedule for teachers who complete additional graduate units after their initial hiring.

Morningstar and Kleinhammer-Tramill (2005) noted that findings from a national survey of special education personnel preparation programs in the United States revealed a lack of quality training in transition preservice training (Anderson et al., 2003) despite the availability of national standards for the preparation for transition specialists (DCDT, 2000). They stated that potential causes of this are 1) decreasing federal funding for transition personnel preparation programs over several years, 2) the collapsing of state special education certification to fewer and broader areas of training (i.e., less personnel preparation time spent on transition services training), and 3) a lack of institutional commitment among higher education to faculty specialization. Clearly there is a need for advanced training in transition services for special education personnel in public schools.

Morningstar and Clark (2003) described five critical knowledge areas with which transition professionals need to be familiar (see Table 4.2). Programs at George Washington University in Washington, D.C., and the University of Kansas in Lawrence, Kansas, two of the most prominent of their kind, offer training in these areas. A brief overview and description of these programs appears in Table 4.3. Both offer traditional on-campus courses as well as online training options. The University of Kansas Transition Certificate program offers an online module specifically focused on transition services for CLD families and youth with disabilities. Another outstanding resource for obtaining advanced training and information about transition services for youth with disabilities is the National Secondary Transition Technical Assistance Center (http://www.nsttac.org). Their web site contains a lot of

Table 4.2.   Five critical areas to cover in transition personnel development

1. *Knowledge of principles and basic concepts of transition education and service*—knowledge and application of transition services requirements under the Individuals with Disabilities Education Improvement Act (IDEA) of 2004 (PL 108-446) as well as emerging and recommended practices focusing on transition planning and individualized education programs

2. *Knowledge of models of transition education and services*—knowledge of specific program models that focus on individualized planning and that align with general secondary education, including models of student-focused planning, student development, family involvement, and interagency collaboration, as described by leaders in the field (Blalock et al., 2003; Division on Career Development and Transition, 2000)

3. *Skills in using strategies for developing, organizing, and implementing transition education and services*—skills needed to implement effective models of transition, as well as transition assessment, service coordination, and curriculum planning within the context of general and special transition instructional programs

4. *Knowledge and use of collaboration competencies*—competence in service coordination with the complex array of agencies, programs, and services supporting young adults with disabilities

5. *Knowledge and skills for addressing systemic problems in transition services delivery*—capacity to understand and address barriers and strategies for planning, developing, implementing, and promoting transition services and programs at local, state, and federal levels. The focus is at the programmatic structural and systems level (Kohler, 1998)

evidence-based information about improving the quality of transition services for families and youth with disabilities.

Interview with Dr. Kristen Powers: The Role of Higher Education in Training School Personnel in Culturally Responsive Transition Planning

I conducted an interview with Dr. Kristen Powers, Professor of School Psychology at California State University, Long Beach, on the role of higher education for training special education and transition services personnel in culturally responsive transition planning. Dr. Powers has been involved in a number of research projects that have investigated the quality of transition services provided to CLD families of youth with disabilities. In addition, she worked as a school psychologist in the public schools for many years. Dr. Powers provides graduate-level training to school psychologists who plan to work in CLD communities in Southern California, most of whom will be involved in transition planning meetings with families and youth with disabilities in the future.

What is your background and training for collaborating with CLD populations, particularly those with special needs at the high school level?

My brothers are adopted; both have disabilities and both come from culturally diverse backgrounds. My Native American brother has emotional disabilities and is currently living independently in a residential setting and has become visually impaired as a result of some unfortunate circumstances which occurred when he spent time in the criminal justice system. My African American brother was born with fetal alcohol syndrome and had a learning disability all through school. He was mainstreamed very little and spent most of his time in special day classrooms; he had great special education teachers. He struggled with his black identity in high school living with us, a white family. He's now out on his own.

> "We need to talk to CLD families of youth with disabilities about the transition planning process and ways that we can increase their participation. Let them talk and we just listen to what they have to say" (Dr. Kristen Powers, personal communication, August 11, 2010).

Table 4.3. Noteworthy graduate programs in transition services

University of Kansas (KU) (Lawrence)

The KU Department of Special Education offers graduate degree programs focusing on transition education and services.

KU Transition Certificate Program (online)

The KU Transition Certificate (KU TransCert) is a nondegree graduate certificate program. This online training program provides a series of transition coursework for secondary special education professionals. Completion of the coursework series leads to a KU graduate certificate in transition. The KU TransCert Program consists of four online transition courses plus a 3-credit culminating experience for a total of 15 graduate credit hours.

Transition Education and Services Master of Science in Education

The Master of Science in Education with an emphasis in Transition Education and Services, a 30-credit-hour graduate program, will soon be offered online. A minimum of 15 hours of the master's program must be met from the approved transition core or elective courses.

Doctoral Program in Secondary Special Education and Transition

This program is designed to provide students with the knowledge and skills necessary to address the complexity of today's policies and practices related to secondary education service provision, special education transition services, community and adult systems, and the needs of underserved populations. This program includes coursework in major and minor areas of doctoral study, as well as opportunities for field-based internship experiences at local, state, and national levels.

For more information, please contact Dr. Mary E. Morningstar, mmorningstar@ku.edu

George Washington (GW) University (Washington, D.C.): Transition Special Education

Graduate School of Education & Human Development

Graduate Certificate, Master of Arts in Education & Human Development (M.A., Ed.H.D.)

Program Overview: The program is designed in partnership with various area public schools and community agencies. The curriculum reflects an interdisciplinary and collaborative approach that emphasizes linking school, community, and postsecondary systems. Specific areas of emphasis are acquired brain injury, collaborative vocational evaluation, learning disabilities, and students with emotional and behavioral disabilities.

One track within the master's program prepares students for special education teacher licensure. A master's degree track that does not include teacher licensure is offered for individuals who are providing an array of disability-focused services for adolescents and adults. Each track offers intensive professional practice through supervised internships in school and community-based settings.

The master's program in transition special education also offers an emphasis in acquired brain injury.

Contact: Dr. Mike Ward, drmikeward@verizon.net; **Dr. Pam Leconte,** pleconte@gwu.edu, (202) 994-1534; **Dr. Carol Kochhar-Bryant,** kochhar@gwu.edu, (202) 994-1536

I became aware of the issues faced by CLD families of youth with disabilities mostly through my research as opposed to practicing school psychology. I feel school psychologists have overlooked the importance of transition planning. We need to talk to CLD families of youth with disabilities about the transition planning process and ways that we can increase their participation. Let them talk and we just listen to what they have to say. We should hold meetings in more flexible ways with respect to when and where we meet. We should use interpreters, ones who are well trained and can reflect the parents' thoughts and concerns. The interpreters should be bicultural and capable of giving good eye contact with the family during the process. We should also gather input from extended family members. Native American families, for example, are very fluid.

What do you feel is needed by teachers in today's schools in order to successfully collaborate with CLD families and youth with disabilities?

I think the first step is awareness of one's own worldview, biases, and the schools in which [one works]. Teachers need to have knowledge of the families with whom they are working with respect to the families' views on disability, parenting, development, developmental landmarks, and milestones in the child's life (e.g., *Quinceañera* for Mexican American girls). Teachers need to know culturally defined views of the term *success.* What does this mean within the context of the culture of the family? What outcomes do they define as success for their child? Data should be presented to teachers as a social justice issue. Have CLD kids with disabilities do testimonials for teachers, talking about their lives.

We should work collectively to solve the problem by building teams. Teams should consist of representatives from across the spectrum. This should include teachers, parents, students, administrators, and district-level personnel. The process should include identifying goals, mapping action steps, training and implementation, and data collection. Identify the resources that can be used to support this process.

What resources and materials can you recommend for accomplishing this leadership training?

OSEP [Office of Special Education Programs] model demonstration grants from the federal government are one possibility. Grants are also available from various community foundations and other nonprofit groups. School districts can contract outside consultants for services. The problem, however, is what to do when the soft money runs out. You can't wait for grants to make a change; many times these efforts are nonsustainable after the grant money runs out. More has to come from leadership within the school district than from outside sources.

Training for teachers should start small and focus on one system at a time—the school, or unit, or district.

What do you feel are the best approaches for providing teacher leadership training in order to promote organizational change in the public schools with respect to the transition of CLD youth with disabilities?

I think we need to begin by raising awareness. We need to make a case for the importance of being aware of the problems faced by CLD families of youth with disabilities in the transition planning process. We should collect the data, present the data, and show evidence of the problem to those we are training. The data [need] to be objective, measurable, and at a school-district level so that [they promote] a sense of desire in teachers for social justice. The typical teacher leadership training model of professional development, which has been referred to as *train and pray,* has not been successful at promoting organizational change in the schools. We need to do more than that.

Others echo many of the thoughts of Dr. Kristen Powers on the role of higher education in providing teacher training on CLD populations. For example, in their article "Developing Responsive Teachers: A Challenge for a Demographic Reality," Garcia, Arias, Murri, and Serna (2010) discussed the role of teacher training in the development of culturally responsive teachers at Arizona State University. They recommended that teacher trainees 1) know about the lives and backgrounds of their students (e.g., families, communities, the effect of home culture on school outcomes); 2) adopt a curriculum that demonstrates an understanding of how CLD students construct knowledge (e.g., connection among language, culture, and identity); 3) develop sociocultural consciousness (e.g., become aware of sociocultural factors situated in communities, classrooms, and schools); and

4) know how to create culturally responsive classrooms, engage in culturally responsive instruction, and demonstrate cultural sensitivity to their students. Garcia et al. (2010) advocated for the use of university–school partnerships and collaboration in supporting teacher preparation in CLD communities. In addition to the tradition of having student teachers work with university supervisors, schools can use university leadership institutes and leader certification to develop culturally responsive practices in teachers.

Maude et al. (2002) described a similar culturally responsive teacher training program (the Crosswalks Intervention) funded by the U.S. Department of Education and implemented by a partnership of six major universities across the country. "The Crosswalks Intervention was developed as a systematic support for teacher preparation programs to become more intentional about, respectful and reflective of, and responsive to cultural and linguistic diversity as part of coursework, field experiences, and program practices" (p. 104). The program provides teacher trainees and practicing teachers with opportunities to explore their own cultural knowledge and awareness and to be exposed to diverse cultural views through direct experience. Participants engage in "an intentional sequence of professional development focused on the evaluation and redesign of course content instructional strategies, field experiences, and collaboration (e.g., with family members and community partners)" (p. 106). The training program includes 1) a 2-day needs assessment of participants, 2) professional development activities on campus, 3) ongoing consultation by phone or e-mail, 4) mini-grants of $500 each to support the acquisition of new instructional resources for increasing an emphasis on diversity, 5) a series of seven full-day face-to-face faculty workshops on various topics related to CLD diversity, 6) an electronic newsletter sent each month to participants, and 7) a searchable database of evidence-based resources related to cultural and linguistic diversity.

Summary of the Promotion of Teacher Leadership in the Public Schools

This section describes a variety of methods for developing leadership skills in special education and transition personnel responsible for providing transition services to CLD families of youth with disabilities. Most of these strategies come from within the school system. The teacher empowerment approach involves principals being willing to share leadership and decision-making powers with their teaching staff. Professional development, a traditional approach to encouraging teacher leadership, must be designed in such a way as to prevent train-and-pray outcomes or the greenhouse effect with teacher trainees. The use of PLCs is a relatively new method of helping teachers exert leadership to affect the instructional quality of their classrooms, schools, and school districts. The focus of PLCs is on teacher inquiry, accountability, data gathering, and data-based decision making by teachers to improve the quality of learning in their students. Action research involves teachers acting as researchers to investigate and solve problems associated with their own practice. Action research, like PLCs, requires teachers to gather data and use these data to make decisions that lead to improvements in the school. Finally, continuing higher education, another traditional approach to supporting teacher leadership, is used to promote advancement in the knowledge and skills of teaching staff. It is based on the belief that being better trained and more informed will translate into teachers having improved practices and leadership skills in their schools and classrooms.

WHAT STRATEGIES CAN BE USED BY TEACHER LEADERS TO PROMOTE ORGANIZATIONAL CHANGE IN THEIR SCHOOLS OR DISTRICTS?

What can teachers do when they see things in their school or district that need to be changed or improved? Teachers sometimes feel that they are nothing more than small fish in a big pond and that they have little to no influence over changing the conditions in which they teach. This frustration has no doubt increased in the past decade considering all of the external initiatives driving public education, such as school reform, high-stakes standardized testing, and the call for nationalized learning and curriculum standards. Teachers can and do make a difference.

In addition to the teacher leadership and empowerment strategies discussed in this chapter, I discovered a number of highly effective organizational change strategies through my own research in the 1980s when pursuing my administrative services credential and my doctorate in special education. These strategies have withstood the test of time and remain highly applicable today. Before I present them, let me offer some background information as to how I discovered them.

I began my RSP career in 1977 teaching students with learning disabilities in a year-round public elementary school of more than 800 students. This was shortly after the passage of the Education for All Handicapped Children Act of 1975 (PL 94-142). One of the major requirements of this legislation was to mainstream students with disabilities into the least restrictive environment, which was considered to be the general education classroom. The law did permit students with learning disabilities to be pulled out of the mainstream for a certain portion of their day to receive specialized services in a RSP classroom, but the majority of their instructional day had to be in a general education classroom. It was my desire to provide specialized services to my students as much as possible in the mainstream (i.e., general education classroom) through co-teaching with the general education teacher instead of pulling the students out to receive services exclusively in the RSP classroom. The problem I faced in attempting to do this was that my predecessor had implemented RSP services exclusively on a pull-out basis.

One of the required courses for my administrative services credential involved completing a fieldwork project, similar to conducting action research. I discussed with my administrative services credential program advisor the problem of having to pull my students out of the general education classroom to receive RSP services. I proposed to develop and conduct staff development with general education teachers on the topic "Successful Mainstreaming: Only You Can Make It Happen!" To my surprise, he was not particularly in favor of this idea because he felt that my proposed solution did not focus on the critical attribute associated with the problem. I subsequently asked him to enlighten me. He told me that the true problem I was facing was how to go about successfully promoting organizational change; my in-service training idea was a simple solution to a much more complex problem. He then encouraged me to conduct my field study (my action research project) on finding out the most effective ways to promote organizational change in the public schools. The idea intrigued me and led to a qualitative study in which I interviewed six highly effective public school leaders (e.g., school superintendents, school principals, a director of special education, special education program specialists) in my

Strategies and solutions for promoting organizational change must focus on the critical attribute associated with the problem in order to be useful and successful.

Table 4.4. Strategies for promoting organizational change

1. Establish a trusting relationship with employees prior to expecting change.
2. Gain staff input into all aspects of change.
3. Utilize the expertise of key, respected leaders in the organization.
4. Promote change initially in small steps.
5. Recruit and hire growth-oriented, enthusiastic employees who are likely to support change.
6. Share the agenda, evidence, and expectations for change with employees.
7. Provide employees with training to develop new skills.
8. Actively confront employees' fear of change.
9. Invite people to change rather than force them to change.
10. Match the change strategy to the unique organization.
11. Do not change for the sake of changing.
12. Change or pay the price.
13. Influence the influencers.
14. Provide resources to support change.
15. Promote personal development in employees to promote change.

school region to determine productive ways to promote organizational change in their employees. Table 4.4 lists the strategies they shared with me.

Several of these strategies correspond to ones cited in the literature on teacher leadership. These include 1) establishing a trusting relationship with employees (e.g., Lieberman et al., 1988, characterized teacher leaders as individuals who engage in building trust and rapport); 2) gaining staff input into all aspects of change and utilizing the expertise of key, respected leaders in the organization (e.g., both of these are key components of PLCs); 3) matching the change strategy to the unique organization (e.g., PLCs promote organizational change by using teacher expertise from within the school rather than external sources); 4) providing employees with training to develop new skills (e.g., professional development); 5) promoting personal development in employees to promote change (e.g., professional development, action research); and 6) providing resources to support change (e.g., this was mentioned by Terry, 2007, as necessary for creating a supportive environment for promoting teacher leadership and empowerment).

A few of the strategies are unique to my experiences and do not directly correspond to recommendations from the published literature on teacher leadership. They are nevertheless very valuable organizational change strategies. One of these is the notion of promoting change initially in small steps. This is a very valuable strategy and one that is akin to the notion of pilot testing. It is wise to implement change in small steps, gathering evaluative data along the way that can be used for revising and improving the specific change in order to determine its long-term effectiveness. This is a key component of action research. If the change works, use it. If it does not work, revise it, try it again, and keep trying until either it is successful or it can be thrown out. Regardless, try something out on a small scale prior to implementing it with the entire population. An example of this in the context of transition planning is to conduct one or two MAPS or engage in other person-centered transition planning methods with a few CLD families of youth with disabilities and analyze the effectiveness of the results before engaging in the process with all CLD families of youth with disabilities at the school.

Another strategy for organizational change in Table 4.4 based on my unpublished qualitative study of effective school leaders is one I call "influencing the influencers." This strategy is similar to the strategy of using the expertise of key, respected leaders in the organization. I used the influencing the influencers strategy when I was trying to promote mainstreaming in my school more than 30 years ago. My school principal and I discussed which general education teachers were highly respected by other teachers on the staff and might be most willing to try co-teaching. I approached these teachers and began the organizational change process with them. Gradually, as they started having success in the classroom, the word spread to other teachers of the value of having an RSP teacher help struggling learners in the mainstream. Eventually I received requests from additional teachers to provide similar support and assistance to their students through a co-teaching role. Special education and transition personnel interested in creating a more culturally responsive transition IEP process can use the same strategy with CLD families of youth with disabilities. Seek out the most influential special education teachers in the school or district and start the change process with them, using any of the many recommendations presented in this book.

Several of the strategies in Table 4.4 appear to contradict one another. For example, change or pay the price seems to be the exact opposite of do not change for the sake of changing. With respect to the latter strategy, one should always examine the pros and cons of any proposed change and attempt to make an informed, data-based decision rather than just go with the flow. Teachers have a professional responsibility to their students, parents, administrators, and school community to provide the highest quality educational services possible. Changing as a result of making an informed, data-based decision is more valid than changing for the sake of changing. With respect to change or pay the price, this strategy, though seemingly negative in tone, is actually based on sound wisdom. Consider the increase in the use of special education attorneys and legal advocates by parents in the public schools since the 1990s. School districts that failed in the past to promote effective organizational change in their special education services and programs are now paying a stiff price. I am concerned that school districts that fail to implement culturally responsive transition planning practices with CLD families of youth with disabilities may face similar consequences in the future. This was one of my primary motivations for writing this book.

Two other strategies in Table 4.4 that appear to contradict one another are actively confronting employees' fear of change and inviting people to change rather than forcing them to do so. Yet these two strategies actually go hand in hand. I definitely recommend starting by inviting people to change rather than forcing them to do so. An elementary school principal for whom I worked for 9 years, Gene Bedley, was awarded National Principal of the Year by the National PTA. One of my favorite expressions of his was "You catch more flies with honey!" This expression corresponds nicely to the organizational change strategy of inviting people to change rather than forcing them to do so. Inviting people to change and simultaneously sharing the agenda, evidence, and expectations for change can facilitate employees sharing their fear of change. This provides the change agent the opportunity to discuss employees' fears directly and offer support and assistance to them in implementing the recommended changes. This requires diplomacy and a certain degree of sophistication on the part of the change agent. Consider again the principal of Alvarado High School described in the case study earlier in this chapter. He requested that Jamie Gutierrez, the special education teacher, present evidence that the transition IEP process at the high school was not culturally responsive to CLD families of youth with disabilities. Jaime was able to produce this evidence and the principal responded, "I can see, Jaime, that you've done your homework. I share your concern that the special education team as a whole may not be as capable as you in terms of working with CLD families to create culturally responsive transition IEPs." Given the strategies in Table 4.4, the next step for this school principal is to speak to other special education and transition personnel in the school either individually or as a group. He should share with them the data, agenda, and expectations for developing a more culturally responsive transition IEP process at Alvarado High School and invite them to be involved in making this happen. He should subsequently listen to his teachers' concerns (i.e., fears of change) and consider possible resources and supports to help them make the necessary changes (e.g., formulation of a PLC, professional development, action research projects).

Finally, the principal at Alvarado High School and Jaime Gutierrez should consider an organizational change strategy listed in Table 4.4 that has yet to be discussed: recruiting and hiring growth-oriented, enthusiastic employees who are likely to support change. This is an excellent change strategy if implemented with care and sensitivity. Teachers come and go for various reasons (e.g., retirement, change of schools within a district, relocation). Recruiting and hiring professionals who support an agenda of change is wise administration and leadership. Jaime Gutierrez should be a key member of a team of professionals who recruit new special education teachers for Alvarado High School if future positions become available. The team should ask candidates about their knowledge and experience in culturally responsive collaboration in the interview or ask that individuals address this in their cover letter when applying for the position.

In summary, the organizational change strategies discussed in this section were derived from expert leaders in the field of education and represent their collective years of knowledge and experience. The strategies are logical and make sense. When appropriately and effectively implemented in practice by teacher leaders, these strategies can and do result in positive organizational change.

SUMMARY

Teachers are the heart and soul of public education. Despite the ongoing challenges they face from both within and outside the education system, they can and do make a difference. Promoting the concept of teachers as leaders is one of the best ways of promoting positive and sustained change and improvement in schools. There is a clear need for change in the transition planning process and transition outcomes achieved by CLD youth with disabilities. Teachers who are familiar with this unique special education student population are perhaps the best qualified to lead this effort. It is unlikely that transition for CLD youth with disabilities will improve without teacher leadership in this area.

This chapter has discussed the characteristics associated with effective teacher leadership as well as the ways in which schools can create supportive environments for creating teacher leaders. Principals should share their power with teachers in ways that allow teachers to feel a sense of ownership and control over the direction of their schools. Empowering teachers allows principals to shift from prescribing solutions to problems to facilitating the discovery of solutions by teachers themselves. Teacher empowerment is needed in schools in order to address the challenges faced by CLD youth with disabilities and their families in the transition planning process during the high school years.

Professional development, also known as *staff development,* is another strategy for developing teacher leadership. Quality professional development requires careful research, planning, implementation, and follow-up in order to be successful and to avoid train-and-pray or greenhouse effect outcomes. Staff development to promote better culturally responsive transition planning in special education teachers working with CLD youth with disabilities and their families is highly recommended.

Many school districts across the country are using PLCs to promote teacher leadership. This approach focuses on creating teacher leadership teams to investigate school problems, collaborate on and propose potential solutions, and gather and analyze data to determine the effectiveness of interventions that have been implemented. Schools should consider the creation of PLCs to investigate and potentially solve some of the problems faced by CLD youth with disabilities and their families in the transition years in high school and beyond.

A similar process is action research, which is implemented by individual teachers and typically focuses on problems within their own classrooms and the learning outcomes of their own students. Like PLCs, action research uses a systematic approach to studying a problem that includes generating key questions, developing and testing potential solutions, gathering and analyzing data, and repeating this process on a cyclical, ongoing basis. Individual teachers interested in studying ways to improve transition planning and outcomes for CLD youth with disabilities are encouraged to engage in action research. Results of their investigations should subsequently be shared with colleagues to promote improvements in the schools for providing transition services to these students and their families.

Continuing higher education, another approach for promoting teacher leadership in schools, is distinguished by the fact that it is based on external resources (i.e., resources outside of the school system versus within it). Many colleges and universities offer CEUs and degree programs for teachers desiring advanced leadership training. Teachers are often rewarded with pay increases for completing continuing higher education classes. College and university programs that partner with local school districts to offer continuing education and leadership training are highly effective at advancing teachers' knowledge and skill. Teachers should investigate college and university programs in their local region that offer programs focusing on ways to promote quality education to CLD populations.

Finally, in this chapter I shared a number of organizational change strategies derived from research I did during my graduate studies. These strategies are ones that effective public school leaders had used to promote positive change in their schools and organizations. All of the strategies are logical, practical, and highly useful. Many of them are similar to other strategies and approaches for developing effective teacher leadership presented elsewhere in this chapter. Teachers and schools should consider adopting many of these strategies in order to promote organizational change that is responsive to the needs of CLD youth with disabilities and their families during the transition years.

In closing, the problems faced by CLD families of youth with disabilities in the transition planning process are not insurmountable. Special education and transition personnel working with these families during the transition years must demonstrate culturally responsive collaboration knowledge and skills.

This chapter has outlined numerous ways in which to develop and promote teacher leadership. A quote from Dr. Bill Beacham is apt: "Change is inevitable. Progress is not." Teacher leadership in the promotion of more culturally responsive transition planning with CLD families and youth with disabilities is critical for progress to occur. There is no time like the present!

5

Epilogue

What Do We Know, What Have We Learned, and Where Do We Go from Here to Help Culturally and Linguistically Diverse Families and Youth with Disabilities in the Transition Process?

Taisha Mubano, an African American woman in her late 40s, ran into Jemilla Franklin, an old friend, after not having seen her for years. Jemilla asked, "How's your son Jonas doing these days? He's probably graduated high school by now."

"Yes indeed," said Taisha, "and he's doing all right. Thanks for asking."

"That's great to hear," said Jemilla, "I know how many years you struggled trying to get services for him. His autism was a real challenge for you and your family."

Taisha replied, "You know, we finally got some good help for Jonas when he started high school. For the first time, I felt the special education teachers listened to what we had to say and truly tried to help us. And it made a big difference!"

"Really," said Jemilla. "What did they do?"

Taisha said, "Well, when Jonas turned 16, they met with us in our home one night with Jonas there, too; put a big piece of paper up on the wall; and asked us a lot of questions about our hopes, fears, dreams, and goals for Jonas's future. Everybody had a chance to talk, including Jonas, and it just felt good. We really thought they cared about him and wanted to help him be successful in school and in the future."

Jemilla replied, skeptically, "Talk is talk. They always make promises, give you hope—but my experience is that they don't deliver."

"Well, nobody is perfect, but the school really made an effort to follow through on what they said they were going to do. Jonas was given a one-to-one aide to work with him in his general education classes, they had a Best Buddies program to help him make friends, and he got a lot of tutoring and assistance with his classes in high school. They helped him get a job at our neighborhood Target store, and the manager there liked him so much that he hired him after Jonas graduated high school. He works there about 30 hours a week. And they helped us connect with services that would help Jonas as an adult."

"That's fantastic!" said Jemilla. "Where's he living now?"

"He lives with us," replied Taisha, "but his Regional Center counselor is helping him look for a supported living situation in the neighborhood."

"What's that?" asked Jemilla.

"It's semi-independent living, like a group home. Other adults with disabilities live there and staff help care for their needs. We think it's great that Jonas can live nearby but be a bit more independent," said Taisha.

"How does he get to work?" asked Jemilla.

"He takes the bus. They taught him how to use the bus when he was in high school," replied Taisha.

"Wow, that's terrific! Sounds like things actually got taken care of. Well, you give Jonas a big hug from me. It was great to see you," said Jemilla.

The story of Taisha Mubano, a happy and satisfied mother of a young adult with autism, illustrates numerous recommended practices in culturally responsive transition planning presented throughout this book. The purpose of this chapter is to synthesize and review this information and to offer some additional transition resources for CLD families and youth with disabilities. The chapter focuses on answering the following questions:

1. What do we know about the transition experiences of CLD families and youth with disabilities?

2. What have we learned about how to support CLD families of youth with disabilities during the transition years?

3. Where do we go from here? How do we infuse research-validated transition practices and recommendations for working with CLD families and youth with disabilities into public schools and transition service agencies?

WHAT DO WE KNOW ABOUT THE TRANSITION EXPERIENCES OF CLD FAMILIES AND YOUTH WITH DISABILITIES?

Making the transition from school to adult life is challenging for all youth with disabilities, but even more so for those from CLD backgrounds. CLD youth with disabilities and their families experience problems with the transition to adult life beyond disability alone. Chapters 1 and 2 provided an extensive review of the literature on this topic. This research has revealed important things regarding CLD families of youth with disabilities who are involved in the transition planning process and the school and transition personnel who interact with them.

The research has found that many school and transition personnel

1. Do not possess critical knowledge and skills related to the multiple dimensions of cultural and linguistic diversity

2. Do not respect CLD parents and youth with disabilities involved in the transition process

3. Do not acknowledge the hopes and dreams for the future held by CLD families and youth with disabilities

4. Do not engage in culturally responsive collaboration with CLD families and youth with disabilities in a way that makes them feel valued, listened to, and accepted during the transition planning process

Research on CLD families and youth with disabilities has found that many of them

1. Lack knowledge of the legal requirements for transition and a clear understanding of their role and function in transition IEP meetings

2. Experience racial and cultural stereotypes as well as biases from school professionals, which leads them to not actively participate in transition IEP meetings

3. Lack proficiency in English and face immigration issues and fears that affect their active participation in transition IEP meetings

4. Possess a different set of norms and cultural expectations for their child's adult future, which leads them to view transition differently than school and transition personnel

In summary, as presented in the first two chapters of this book, CLD youth with disabilities experience serious problems in the transition process beyond those experienced by youth with disabilities in the general population. Fortunately, an emerging body of literature focusing on this unique population has provided recommendations for how to address this problem.

WHAT HAVE WE LEARNED ABOUT HOW TO SUPPORT CLD FAMILIES OF YOUTH WITH DISABILITIES DURING THE TRANSITION YEARS?

A number of highly effective practices have been recommended to promote more positive transition experiences for CLD families and youth with disabilities. These recommendations apply to two specific groups: 1) school transition professionals and 2) CLD parents and youth with disabilities. Suggestions for transition professionals include the following:

1. Transition professionals need to be competent in culturally responsive collaboration and communication practices that facilitate their ability to effectively engage in skilled dialogue with CLD families and youth with disabilities.

2. School districts and transition service agencies need to assess the quality of knowledge and skills of personnel who collaborate with CLD families and youth with disabilities in transition planning using the instrument presented in the Chapter 2 appendix or a similar instrument.

3. School districts and transition service agencies need to provide cultural competence training to personnel who lack quality knowledge and skills for engaging in culturally responsive collaboration with CLD families and youth with disabilities involved in transition planning.

4. Special education and transition service personnel might consider conducting transition planning with CLD families and youth with disabilities in informal environments, such as the home, instead of in the school or other public settings.

5. Transition professionals should use culturally responsive techniques such as PCP and family-centered approaches to collaborate with CLD families and youth with disabilities.

Here's what we've learned about helping CLD families and youth with disabilities in the transition process.

1. CLD parents who know their rights and responsibilities in formulating postsecondary goals for their child and other aspects of special education law and practice are more active in transition IEP meetings in the public schools and are better able to advocate for their children with disabilities. Therefore, CLD parents and youth with disabilities need to increase their knowledge and skills in these areas.

2. Training is available throughout the United States to promote the knowledge and skills of CLD families and youth with disabilities with respect to not only the transition planning process but all aspects of special education and special education law. Resources for such training are included in the For More Information section of this book, and experts should encourage CLD families of youth with disabilities to access these resources and receive this training.

3. Parent support groups, mentors, and community liaisons benefit CLD parents of youth with disabilities by helping them understand special education law, the special education system in the public schools, and their role in the transition planning process. CLD families and youth with disabilities need to seek out existing resources such as these or create similar ones in their school districts or communities.

4. The use of bilingual and bicultural interpreters who are well trained and knowledgeable in special education law and practice benefits families who do not speak English. CLD parents should request that schools provide these types of interpreters to them throughout the transition planning process.

Interview with Irene Martinez, M.S.W., Director of Fiesta Educativa

I conducted an interview with Irene Martinez, M.S.W., who is the Director of Fiesta Educativa, a parent support organization for CLD parents of youth with disabilities in Los Angeles, California (http://www.fiestaeducativa.org). Many of the questions I asked her were related to the recommended practices just discussed.

What cultures are represented in the CLD population for your service region?

We work with families from East Los Angeles and the San Gabriel Valley. These are primarily Latino and Chinese families.

What challenges have you seen CLD families of youth with disabilities face in the transition planning process?

Many of our Latino families are monolingual Spanish-speaking recent immigrants. They have different levels of acculturation. Some of them are from low-SES backgrounds and are struggling to live day to day. They don't plan ahead. They need prompting. Sometimes the schools don't initiate with these parents, and the parents don't think about transition planning.

Some of the sons or daughters of these families graduate at 18 or 22 years of age and just stay at home. If the families decide to keep them at home, it's for safety and security, not because they want to hide them. The families we've worked with are generally open to resources and services offered. Undocumented status is not a problem; we don't ask them about their immigration status.

What things have you tried and implemented to improve the quality of collaboration with CLD families of youth with disabilities in the transition planning process? What has been successful and what has not?

We have tried to provide more training to parents to get them to start transition planning earlier. We've tried to raise consciousness in them. We have conducted one-to-one workshops. We get referrals from Regional Centers and family resource centers, and from the media where we have done advertising. We have developed good working relationships with a number of school districts in our region, but we're limited by resources. We have written and obtained grants, but there are large pockets of underserved CLD families we have not been able to get to.

We're using a home-based family education model. A small group of parents get together in a host parent's home. It's a family driven and family centered environment that is interactive. We provide speakers and trainers who answer specific questions the families ask. This is one of the most effective models for helping CLD families and youth with disabilities during transition.

We have a professional advisory council. We have a statewide grant that was funded. And we have received foundation funding that led to a contract with three counties to work with Regional Centers. Regional and statewide conferences are another way we have been able to successfully network with CLD parents of youth with disabilities and find resources.

We have a grant from the J.P. Morgan Foundation which we used to form a school district partnership. We met with the school district director of special education initially; the key was to get principals to buy in. We found three schools and sold the idea to the principals. Parent community representative liaisons became involved in the partnership as well. We designed curriculum, workshops, and more formal professionally oriented training. We conducted the workshops in the morning when kids are in school. We sent mail outs, made fliers, and made telephone calls to families to get them to attend. There are six modules, some of which include training on the transition process, IEPs, and behavior. Parents are required to attend all six modules and earn a certificate of completion at the end. We are hoping to add a middle school to the partnership next year.

What do you recommend as best practices for collaborating with CLD families of youth with disabilities in the transition planning process?

Help the parents work with the school so there is not a broken relationship. Help parents be more interactive and facilitate a positive relationship with the school. Parents need to work with the resources they are entitled to for their child who is transition age.

What do the CLD families and youth with disabilities with whom you have worked want and need when it comes to planning the future for their child?

Parents of youth with developmental disabilities need employment development services for their child. They haven't thought about their child working. We need to help them to see their adult children differently; they are fearful of their child going to work.

We provide them with training to help with job development so they can see that they can have control. We try to encourage a strong family component in our training rather than focus on self-advocacy and self-determination. They need to take responsibility for their child and obtain more knowledge of how to work with the IEP team and educational system. They need to learn how the system works, such as the role of Regional Centers and the Department of Rehabilitation in the transition of their child.

What advice and support do you offer to transition professionals who interact with the CLD families and youth with disabilities with whom you work?

Latino families may not be proactive. They need to be informed and encouraged to seek out education opportunities. When they are given this opportunity, they do respond. Offer them training, resources, and opportunities.

What do you think are key strategies to promote leadership and improved services for CLD families of youth with disabilities in your community?

Work with schools. Work with school districts and on-site administrators. Work with local parent council representatives. The family-based home host parent program promotes leadership in these parents. You need to develop parent leadership. Raise consciousness, attend councils and advisory panels, and increase CLD parent involvement in leadership. Help parents to become advocates for their child and promote regional system change and to have influence on public policies.

In this interview, Irene Martinez reinforces many of the practices recommended in the literature for schools to help CLD families of youth with disabilities become more knowledgeable and capable with regard to the transition planning process. The question that remains is where do we go from here? How do we make this happen?

WHERE DO WE GO FROM HERE?

How do we infuse research-validated transition practices and recommendations for working with CLD families and youth with disabilities into public schools and transition service agencies? This is perhaps the biggest challenge that must be faced. Translating research into practice can be a difficult process and often becomes derailed by poor public policy, ineffective implementation of recommended practices, or competing educational or school initiatives. However, there are a number of ways to put into practice the information that has been presented and discussed in this book:

1. Use the leadership strategies presented in Chapter 4 to develop leaders in school special education and transition service agency personnel working with CLD families and youth with disabilities involved in the transition process. Promote similar leadership development in CLD parents of youth with disabilities whose children either have reached adulthood or are transition age. These parents can serve in an advisory capacity to schools or transition service agencies (see the interview with Irene Martinez for some specific suggestions).

2. Select and implement the organizational change strategies discussed in Chapter 4 that would work best with the stakeholders and constituents in the local schools or region.

Implement and evaluate the effectiveness of these strategies for promoting organizational change and improved outcomes for CLD families and youth with disabilities in the transition process.

3. Provide training where training is needed to transition professionals as well as CLD families and youth with disabilities. Use the recommended training format and content presented in Chapter 2 as well as the approaches mentioned by Irene Martinez.

4. Develop resources such as CLD parent support groups, mentors, and community liaisons to help CLD families in the transition process. Contact existing groups and programs that provide these services for recommendations on how to initiate them in the local schools or region (see the list of additional recommended resources for CLD families of youth with disabilities in the For Further Information section).

5. Pursue continuing knowledge, education, and professional growth on this topic to maintain currency in the field. Share this information with others on a consistent and ongoing basis.

6. Seek external funding from nonprofit organizations, grants, and foundations to promote program development and improved practice in this area.

7. Attend local, state, and national conferences to gain further information, resources, and training on this topic and to network with others who have similar interests in this area.

8. Keep your eye on the ball; remain passionate and committed to the process and recognize that change occurs slowly and often requires up to 5–7 years to be fully implemented. Don't give up!

SUMMARY

Everyone deserves an equal opportunity to experience a quality adult life, including individuals with disabilities. CLD families and youth with disabilities involved in the transition process face additional challenges, but professionals can support them effectively through culturally responsive collaboration. This book has included guidance on this collaboration, as well as considerations for making legal and effective transition documents (secondary transition IEPs and SOPs) for CLD youth with disabilities. Yet beyond the direct practices involved with individual families, improvement in support for CLD families of youth with disabilities requires changes at an organizational level. Thus, this book has presented information on how to promote leadership in special education and transition service agency personnel who interact with CLD families and youth with disabilities in the transition process. Experts can use these strategies to improve the schools and agencies in which special education and transition service personnel work.

I wrote this book not only for school and transition service agency personnel but also for CLD families and youth with disabilities involved in the transition process. I wanted to give these individuals a voice by presenting their words, feelings, and experiences related to the transition process. I have presented information and resources aimed at empowering these individuals to better advocate for themselves in the transition process. Moreover, I have attempted to show them how to assume leadership in schools and communities that will result in better and more culturally responsive transition services for other CLD families and youth with disabilities in the future.

The case studies, interviews, resources, and references presented here are not an exhaustive compilation of the research on this subject. However, they represent a solid review of the literature and a balanced presentation of practical and theoretical information about the transition process for CLD youth with disabilities. I invite further research, writing, professional presentations, and professional growth on this topic and hope that this book will inspire others to pursue these directions in the future.

How fortunate Americans are to live in a country that believes in and is committed to providing equal opportunity for all individuals, including those with disabilities. I have dedicated a significant portion of my professional career in education to improving the transition outcomes of youth with disabilities. My hope is that this book will make an additional contribution to this effort, particularly for those youth with disabilities who come from CLD backgrounds.

References

Americans with Disabilities Act of 1990, PL 101-336, 42 U.S.C. §§ 12101 *et seq.*

Anderson, D., Kleinhammer-Tramill, P.J., Morningstar, M.E., Lehmann, J., Bassett, D., Kohler, P., & Wehmeyer, M. (2003). What's happening in personnel preparation in transition? A national survey. *Career Development for Exceptional Individuals, 26,* 145–160.

Barrera, I., & Corso, R.M. (with Macpherson, D.). (2003). *Skilled dialogue: Strategies for responding to cultural diversity in early childhood.* Baltimore: Paul H. Brookes Publishing Co.

Bass, B.M. (1985). *Leadership and performance beyond expectations.* New York: Free Press.

Blackorby, J., & Wagner, M. (1996). Longitudinal postschool outcomes of youth with disabilities: Findings from the National Longitudinal Transition Study. *Exceptional Children, 62,* 399–413.

Blalock, G., Kochhar-Bryant, C., Test, D., Kohler, P., White, W., Lehman, J., et al. (2003). The need for comprehensive personnel preparation in transition and career development: A position statement of the Division on Career Development and Transition. *Career Development for Exceptional Individuals, 26*(2), 207–226.

Blue-Banning, M., Summers, J.A., Frankland, H.C., Nelson, L.L., & Beegle, G. (2004). Dimensions of family and professional partnerships: Constructive guidelines for collaboration. *Exceptional Children, 70,* 167–184.

Bolin, F.S. (1989). Empowering leadership. *Teachers College Record, 91,* 81–96.

Brandon, R.R. (2007). African American parents: Improving connections with their child's educational environment. *Intervention in School and Clinic, 43,* 116–120.

Brandon, R.R., & Brown, M.R. (2009). African American families in the special education process: Increasing their involvement. *Intervention in School and Clinic, 45,* 85–90.

The California Department of Education. (2007). *Transition to adult living: An information and resource guide.* California Services for Technical Assistance and Training (CalSTAT) at the California Institute on Human Services. Rohnert Park, CA: Sonoma State University.

Clark, G.M., Patton, J.R., & Moulton, L.R. (2000). *Informal assessments for transition planning.* Austin, TX: PROD-ED.

Clay, J. (2007). *American Indians and disability: Montana's AIDTAC program.* Missoula, MN: American Indian Disability Technical Assistance Center. University of Montana Rural Institute. Retrieved January 22, 2008, from http://usinfo.state.gov/journals/itsv/1106/ijse/aidtac.htm

Crowther, F. (1997). Teachers as leaders: An exploratory framework. *International Journal of Educational Management, 11*(1), 6–13.

Darling-Hammond, L. (1997). *The right to learn: A blueprint for creating schools that work.* San Francisco: Jossey-Bass.

Darling-Hammond, L., & McLaughlin, M.W. (1995). Policies that support professional development in an era of reform. *Phi Delta Kappan, 76,* 597–604.

Delpit, L. (1995). *Other peoples's children: Cultural conflict in the classroom.* New York: The New Press.

Division on Career Development and Transition. (2000). *Transition specialist competencies: Fact sheet.* Reston, VA: Council for Exceptional Children.

DuFour, R. (2004). What is a "professional learning community"? *Educational Leadership, 61*(8), 1–6.

Dukes, L.L. (2010). Gathering data to determine eligibility for services and accommodations. In S.F. Shaw, J.W. Madaus, & L.L. Dukes (Eds.), *Preparing students with disabilities for college success: A practical guide to transition planning* (pp. 167–190). Baltimore: Paul H. Brookes Publishing Co.

Edgar, E. (1991). Providing ongoing support and making appropriate placements: An alternative to transition planning for mildly handicapped students. *Preventing School Failure, 35*(2), 36–39.

Education for All Handicapped Children Act of 1975, PL 94-142, 20 U.S.C. §§ 1400 *et seq.*

Falvey, M.A., Forest, M., Pearpoint, J., & Rosenburg, R.L. (1997). *All my life's a circle. Using the tools: Circles, MAPS & PATHS.* Toronto, Ontario, Canada: Inclusion Press.

Field, S., & Hoffman, A. (1996). *Steps to self-determination.* Austin, TX: PRO-ED.

Field, S., Martin, J., Miller, R., Ward, M., & Wehmeyer, M. (1988). *Self-determination for persons with disabilities: A position statement of the Division on Career Development and Transition.* Arlington, VA: Council for Exceptional Children.

Furman, G.C., & Shields, C.M. (2003, April). *How can educational leaders promote and support social justice and democratic community in schools?* Paper presented at the annual meeting of the American Educational Research Association, Chicago, IL.

Garcia, E., Arias, M.B., Murri, N.J.H., & Serna, C. (2010). Developing responsive teachers: A challenge for a demographic reality. *Journal of Teacher Education, 61*(1–2), 132–141.

Geenen, S., Powers, L.E., Lopez-Vasquez, A., & Bersani, H. (2003). Understanding and promoting the transition of minority adolescents. *Career Development for Exceptional Individuals, 26,* 27–46.

Gil-Kashiwabara, E., Hogansen, S.G., Geenen, S., Powers, K., & Powers, L. (2007). Improving transition outcomes for marginalized youth. *Career Development for Exceptional Individuals, 30,* 80–91.

Greene, G. (1996). Empowering culturally and linguistically diverse families in the transition planning process. *Journal for Vocational Special Needs Education, 19*(1), 26–30.

Greene, G. (2009). Transition assessment. In C.A. Kochhar-Bryant & G. Greene, *Pathways to successful transition for youth with disabilities: A developmental process* (2nd ed., pp. 236–263). Upper Saddle River, NJ: Merrill/Pearson.

Greene, G., & Kochhar-Bryant, C.A. (2003). *Pathways to successful transition for youth with disabilities.* Upper Saddle River, NJ: Merrill-Prentice Hall.

Halloran, W.D. (1993). Transition services requirement: Issues, implications, and challenges. In R.C. Eaves & P.J. McLaughlin (Eds.), *Recent advances in special education and rehabilitation* (pp. 210–224). Boston: Andover Medical.

Halpern, A.S., Herr, C.M., Wolf, N.K., Doren, B., Johnson, M.D., & Lawson, J.D. (1997). *Next S.T.E.P.: Student transition and educational planning.* Austin, TX: PRO-ED.

Harry, B.H. (1992). *Cultural diversity, families, and the special education system: Communication and empowerment.* New York: Teachers College Press.

Harry, B.H. (2008). Collaboration with culturally and linguistically diverse families: Ideal versus reality. *Exceptional Children, 74,* 327–388.

Harry, B., Allen, N., & McLaughlin, M. (1995). Communication versus compliance: African American parents' involvement in special education. *Exceptional Children, 61,* 364–377.

Hasazi, S.B., Gordon, L.R., & Roe, C.A. (1985). Factors associated with the employment status of handicapped youth exiting high school from 1979–1983. *Exceptional Children, 51,* 455–469.

Individuals with Disabilities Education Act Amendments of 1997, PL 105-17, 20 U.S.C. §§ 1400 *et seq.*

Individuals with Disabilities Education Act (IDEA) of 1990, PL 101-476, 20 U.S.C. §§ 1400 *et seq.*

Individuals with Disabilities Education Improvement Act (IDEA) of 2004, PL 108-446, 20 U.S.C. §§ 1400 *et seq.*

Inger, M. (1992). Increasing the school involvement of Hispanic parents. *ERIC Clearinghouse on Urban Education Digest, 80,* 24–25.

Iowa Model for Transition Assessments. (n.d.). Retrieved August 7, 2010, from http://transitionassessment. northcentralrrc.org/IowaModel.aspx

Jacobson, D. (2010). Coherent instructional improvement and PLCs: Is it possible to do both? *Phi Delta Kappan, 91*(6), 38–45.

Kalyanpur, M., & Harry, B. (1997). A posture of reciprocity: A practical approach to collaboration between professionals and parents of culturally diverse backgrounds. *Journal of Child and Family Studies, 6,* 487–509.

Kalyanpur, M., & Harry, B. (1999). *Culture in special education: Building reciprocal family-professional relationships.* Baltimore: Paul H. Brookes Publishing Co.

Kim, K.H., & Morningstar, M. (2005). Transition planning involving culturally and linguistically diverse families. *Career Development for Exceptional Individuals, 28,* 95–101.

Kochhar-Bryant, C., Bassett, D.S., & Webb, K.W. (2009). *Transition to postsecondary education for students with disabilities.* Thousand Oaks, CA: Corwin Press.

Kochhar-Bryant, C.A., & Greene, G. (2009). *Pathways to successful transition for youth with disabilities: A developmental process* (2nd ed.). Upper Saddle River, NJ: Merrill/Pearson.

Kochhar-Bryant, C.A., & Izzo, M.V. (2006). Access to post-high school services: Transition assessment and the summary of performance. *Career Development for Exceptional Individuals, 29,* 70–89.

Kohler, P. (1998). Implementing a transition perspective of education. In F. Rusch & J. Chadsey (Eds.), *Beyond high school: Transition from school to work* (pp. 179–205). Belmont, CA: Wadsworth Publishing.

Lai, Y., & Ishiyama, F.I. (2004). Involvement of immigrant Chinese Canadian mothers of children with disabilities. *Exceptional Children, 71,* 97–108.

Landmark, L.J., Zhang, D.D., & Montoya, L. (2007). Culturally diverse parents' experiences in the children's transition: Knowledge and involvement. *Career Development for Exceptional Individuals, 30,* 68–79.

Leake, D., & Black, R. (2005). *Essential tools: Improving secondary education and transition for youth with disabilities: Cultural and linguistic diversity: Implications for transition personnel.* Minneapolis, MN: National Center on Secondary Education and Transition.

Leake, D., & Boone, R. (2007). Multicultural perspectives on self-determination from youth, parent, and teacher focus groups. *Career Development for Exceptional Individuals, 30,* 104–115.

Lee, W. (1991). Empowering music teachers: A catalyst for change. *Music Education Journal, 78*(1), 36–39.

Lieberman, A., Saxl, E., & Miles, M. (Eds.). (1988). *Building a professional culture in New York schools.* New York: Teachers College Press.

Liontos, L.B. (1991). *Involving at-risk families in their children's education.* Eugene, OR: ERIC Clearinghouse on Educational Management. (ERIC Document Reproduction Service No. ED326925)

Locust, C. (1988). Wounding the spirit: Discrimination and traditional American Indian belief systems. *Harvard Educational Review, 58*(3), 315–330.

Locust, C. (1994). *The Piki maker: Disabled American Indians, cultural beliefs, and traditional behaviors.* Tucson: AZ: Native American Research Center.

Lucas, S., Brown, G.C., & Marcus, F.W. (1991). Principals' perceptions of site-based management and teacher empowerment. *NASSP Bulletin, 75*(357), 56–62.

Lynch, E.W., & Hanson, M.J. (2004). *Developing cross-cultural competence: A guide for working with children and their families* (3rd ed.). Baltimore: Paul H. Brookes Publishing Co.

Lynch, E.W., & Hanson, M.J. (2011). *Developing cross-cultural competence: A guide for working with children and their families* (4th ed.). Baltimore: Paul H. Brookes Publishing Co.

Martin, J.E., & Marshall, L.H. (1994). *Choicemaker self-determination transition curriculum matrix.* Colorado Springs: University of Colorado Center for Educational Research.

Maude, S.P., Catlett, C., Moore, S., Sanchez, S.Y., Thorp, E.K., & Corso, R. (2002). Infusing diversity constructs in preservice teacher preparation: The impact of a systematic faculty development strategy. *Infants & Young Children, 32*(2), 103–121.

Mertler, C.A. (2009). *Action research: Teachers as researchers in the classroom* (2nd ed.). Thousand Oaks, CA: Sage.

Miller, R.J., Lombard, R.C., & Corbey, S.A. (2007). *Transition assessment: Planning transition and IEP development for youth with mild to moderate disabilities.* Boston: Allyn & Bacon.

Mills, G.E. (2007). *Action research: A guide for the teacher researcher* (3rd ed.). Upper Saddle River, NJ: Merrill/Prentice Hall.

Morningstar, M.E., & Clark, G.M. (2003). The status of personnel preparation for transition education and services: What is the critical content? How can it be offered? *Career Development for Exceptional Individuals, 26,* 227–237.

Morningstar, M.E., & Kleinhammer-Tramill, J. (2005). *Professional development for transition personnel: Current issues and strategies for success* (Information Brief Vol. 4, No. 4). Minneapolis, MN: National Center on Secondary Education and Transition.

Morrisey, M., Cowan, D., Leo, T., & Blair, L. (1999). Renewing teachers reforming schools through professional learning communities. *SED Letter, 11*(2), 8–11.

Murphy, J. (2002). Reculturing the profession of educational leadership: New blueprints. *Educational Administration Quarterly, 38,* 176–191.

National Council on Disability. (2003). *National disability policy: A progress report: December 2001–December 2002.* Retrieved from http://www.ncd.gov/newsroom/publications/2003/progressreport_final.htm

National Longitudinal Transition Study–2. (2005). *Changes over time in postschool outcomes of youth with disabilities.* Retrieved from http://nlts2.org/pdfs/str6_completereport.pdf

National Transition Documentation Summit (2005). www.cec.sped.org/AM/Template.cfm?Section=Search &TEMPLATE=/CM/ContentDisplay.cfm&CONTE NTID=6031

National Secondary Transition Technical Assistance Center (http://www.nsttac.org).

Newman, L., Wagner, M., Cameto, R., & Knokey, A.-M. (2009). *The post-high school outcomes of youth with disabilities up to 4 years after high school: A report of findings from the National Longitudinal Transition Study-2 (NLTS2)* (NCSER Report No. 2009-3017). Menlo Park, CA: SRI International. Retrieved from www.nlts2.org/reports/2009_04/nlts2_report_2009_04_complete.pdf

O'Hair, M.J., McLaughlin, H.J., & Reitzug, U.C. (2000). *Foundations of democratic education*. Orlando, FL: Harcourt.

Olivos, E.M. (2009). Collaboration with Latino families: A critical perspective of home-school interactions. *Intervention in School and Clinic, 45*, 109–115.

Pewewardy, C., & Fitzpatrick, M. (2009). Working with American Indian students and families: Disabilities, issues, and interventions. *Intervention in School and Clinic, 45*, 92–98.

Pounder, J.S. (2006). Transformational classroom leadership. *Educational Management Administration & Leadership, 34*, 533–545.

Povenmire-Kirk, T.C., Lindstrom, L., & Bullis, M. (2010). De escuela a la vida adulta [Transition needs for Latino youth with disabilities]. *Career Development for Exceptional Individuals, 33*(1), 25–40.

Powers, L.E., Ellison, R., Matuszewski, J., Wilson, R., & Turner, A. (1997). *Take charge for the future*. Portland, OR: Health Sciences University, Center on Self-Determination.

Rehabilitation Act Amendments of 1998, PL 105-220, 29 U.S.C. §§ 701 *et seq.*

Rehabilitation Act of 1973, PL 93-112, 29 U.S.C. §§ 701 *et seq.*

Reitzug, U.C. (1991). A case study of empowering principal behavior. *American Educational Research Journal, 31*, 238–307.

Reitzug, U.C., & O'Hair, M.J. (2002). Tensions and struggles in moving toward a democratic school community. In G.C. Furman (Ed.), *School as community* (pp. 119–141). Albany: State University of New York Press.

Remen, R.N. (2000). *My grandfather's blessings*. New York: Riverhead Books.

Rueda, R., Monzo, L., Shapiro, J., Gomez, J., & Blacher, J. (2005). Cultural models of transition: Latina mothers of young adults with disabilities. *Exceptional Children, 71*, 401–414.

Salembier, G., & Furney, K.S. (1997). Facilitating participation: Parents' perceptions of their involvement in IEP/transition planning process. *Career Development for Exceptional Individuals, 20*, 29–42.

Shaw, S., Kochhar-Bryant, C., Izzo, M., Benedict, K., & Parker, D. © 2005 National Transition Documentation Summit.

Silva, D.Y., Gimbert, B., & Nolan, J. (2000). Sliding the doors: Locking and unlocking possibilities for teacher leadership. *Teachers College Record, 102*, 779–804.

Singer, G.H.S., & Powers, L.C. (1993). Contributing to resilience in families: An overview. In G.H.S. Singer & L.C. Powers (Eds.), *Families, disability, and empowerment: Active coping skills and strategies for family interventions* (pp. 1–25). Baltimore: Paul H. Brookes Publishing Co.

Sitlington, P.L., & Clark, G.M. (2006). *Transiton education and services for students with disabilities* (4th ed., p. 134). Boston: Pearson/Allyn & Bacon.

Sitlington, P.L., Neubert, D.A., Begun, W., Lombard, R.C., & Leconte, P.J. (1996). *Assess for success: Handbook on transition assessment*. Arlington, VA: Council for Exceptional Children.

Sitlington, P.L., Neubert, D.A., & Leconte, P.J. (1997). Transition assessment: The position of the Division on Career Development and Transition. *Career Development for Exceptional Individuals, 20*, 69–79.

Smith, D.D., & Tyler, N.C. (2010). *Introduction to special education: Making a difference*. Upper Saddle River, NJ: Merrill/Pearson.

Terry, P.M. (2007). Empowering teachers as leaders. *National FORUM Journals*. Retrieved from http://www.nationalforum.com/Electronic%20Journal%20Volumes/Terry,%20paul%20M.%20Empowering%20Teachers%20As%20Leaders.pdf

Test, D.W., Aspel, N.P., & Everson, J.M. (2006). *Transition methods for youth with disabilities*. Upper Saddle River, NJ: Pearson.

Trainor, A.A. (2007). Person-centered planning in two culturally distinct communities: Responding to divergent needs and preferences. *Career Development for Exceptional Individuals, 30*, 92–103.

Trueba, H., & Delgado-Gaitan, C. (1988). *Minority achievement and parental support: Academic resocialization through mentoring*. Santa Barbara: University of California.

U.S. Census Bureau. (2001). United States Census 2000. Unpublished raw data.

Valenzuela, R.L., & Martin, J. (2005). Self-directed IEP: Bridging values of diverse cultures and secondary education. *Career Development for Exceptional Individuals, 28*, 4–14.

Van Reusen, A.K., & Bos, C.S. (1990). I plan: Helping students communicate in planning conferences. *Teaching Exceptional Children, 22*(4), 30–2.

Vandercook, T., & York, J. (1989). The McGill Action Planning System (M.A.P.S.): A strategy for building vision. *Journal of The Association for Persons with Severe Handicaps, 14,* 205–215.

Wehman, P. (1996). *Life beyond the classroom: Transition strategies for young people with disabilities.* Baltimore: Paul H. Brookes Publishing Co.

Wehman, P. (2006). *Life beyond the classroom: Transition strategies for young people with disabilities* (4th ed.). Baltimore: Paul H. Brookes Publishing Co.

Wehman, P. (2011). *Essentials of transition planning.* Baltimore: Paul H. Brookes Publishing Co.

Wehman, P., & Wittig, K.M. (2009). *Transition IEPs: A curriculum guide for teachers and transition practitioners.* Austin, TX: PRO-ED.

Wehmeyer, M.L., & Kelchner, K. (1995). *Whose future is it anyway? Student-directed transition planning program.* Austin, TX: The Arc of the United States.

Williams, L., Cate, J., & O'Hair, M.J. (2009). The boundary-spanning role of democratic learning communities: Implementing the IDEALS. *Educational Management Administration & Leadership, 37,* 452–472.

For Further Information

Publications

DeFur, S.H., Todd-Allen, M., & Getzel, E.E. (2001). Parent participation in the transition planning process. *Career Development for Exceptional Individuals, 24*(1), 19–36.

This article presents the research behind a model designed to evaluate and develop effective practices for involving families in the transition planning process based on the insights gained from this study and the existing literature.

Dukes, C., & Lamar-Dukes, P. (Eds.). (2009). Diversity: What we know, what we need to know, *and what we need to do. [Special Issue]. Research and Practice for Persons with Severe Disabilities, 34*(3–4).

This special issue of the TASH journal addresses a range of issues related to diversity and people with intellectual and developmental disabilities.

Hasnain, R., Kondratowicz, D.M., Borokhovski, E., Nye, C., Balcazar, F., Portillo, N., et al. (2011). Do cultural competency interventions work? A systematic review on improving rehabilitation outcomes for ethnically and linguistically diverse individuals with disabilities. *FOCUS Technical Brief, 31.* Austin, TX: SEDL, National Center for the Dissemination of Disability Research.

This issue describes a systematic review conducted to determine whether cultural competency interventions improve rehabilitation outcomes for ethnically and linguistically diverse individuals with disabilities, and if so, for whom and under what conditions.

Martin, J.E., Marshall, L.H., Maxson, L.M., & Jerman, P.L. (1996). *The self-directed IEP.* Longmont, CO: Sopris West.

The Self-Directed IEP is a multimedia package that teaches students how to participate in, and even lead, their own individualized education program (IEP) meetings. The IEP process provides an excellent opportunity for students in special education to learn self-determination skills, which are important in successful postschool transition.

Munk, D.D., & Dempsey, T.L. (2010). *Leadership strategies for successful schoolwide inclusion: The STAR Approach.* Baltimore: Paul H. Brookes Publishing Co.

This concise book gives principals and other school leaders the solution they've been waiting for: a clear framework for leading inclusion efforts, monitoring their success, and facilitating consistent use of best practices in all facets of planning for students with disabilities.

Stanberry, K. (2010). *Transition planning for students with IEPs: Life after school.* Retrieved from http://www.greatschools.org/special-education/health/873-transition-planning-for-students-with-ieps.gs?page=1

GreatSchools is the country's leading source of information on school performance. This article shows how this part of the IEP allows a teen in special education to outline goals that will help him achieve his post–high school plans.

Test, D.W., & Algozzine, B. (Eds.). (2007). [Special issue]. *Career Development for Exceptional Individuals, 30*(2).

This special issue, published by the DCDT, a division of the Council for Exceptional Children, addresses the topic of transition of CLD youth with disabilities and their families.

Trainor, A.A. (in press). Multicultural transition planning: Including all youth with disabilities. In Wehman, P., *Life beyond the classroom: Transition strategies for young people with disabilities* (5th ed.). Baltimore, Paul H. Brookes Publishing Co.

This chapter provides readers with considerations when planning for post-school outcomes for students with a range of disabilities.

Trainor, A.A. (2008). Using cultural and social capital to improve postsecondary outcomes and expand transition models for youth with disabilities. *Journal of Special Education, 42,* 148–162.

This article addresses the attention dedicated to the forms of capital possessed by young adults with disabilities or to teachers' expectations of the role of capital in achieving postsecondary outcomes. Studies of capital inform postsecondary transition research and practice in key areas including self-determination, parent participation, access to appropriate curriculum, and linkages to adult services.

Organizations

ALLIANCE National Parent Technical Assistance Center

http://www.parentcenternetwork.org

The ALLIANCE provides innovative technical assistance, up-to-date information, and high quality resources and materials. A major goal of the ALLIANCE is to build the capacity of Parent Centers in order to improve results for children with disabilities of all ages in rural, urban, and suburban areas and from underrepresented and underserved populations.

American Translators Association

http://www.atanet.org/onlinedirectories/

ATA is a professional association founded to advance the translation and interpreting professions and foster the professional development of individual translators and interpreters. This online directory features the profiles of more than 6,000 translators and interpreters. Each listing provides the individual's language, location, specialties, experience, and contact information.

APSE

http://www.apse.org

APSE is a growing national nonprofit membership organization founded in 1988 and formerly known as the Association for Persons in Supported Employment. It is the *only* national organization with an *exclusive focus* on integrated employment and career advancement opportunities for individuals with disabilities.

The Arc of the United States

http://www.thearc.org

The Arc is the world's largest community-based organization of and for people with intellectual and developmental disabilities. It provides an array of services and supports for families and individuals and includes more than 140,000 members affiliated through more than 730 state and local chapters across the nation. The Arc is devoted to promoting and improving supports and services for all people with intellectual and developmental disabilities.

Association for Higher Education and Disability (AHEAD)

http://www.ahead.org

AHEAD is a professional membership organization for individuals involved in the development of policy and in the provision of quality services to meet the needs of persons with disabilities involved in all areas of higher education.

Council for Exceptional Children (CEC)

http://www.cec.sped.org

CEC is the largest international professional organization dedicated to improving the educational success of individuals with disabilities and/or gifts and talents. CEC advocates for appropriate governmental policies, sets professional standards, provides professional development, advocates for individuals with exceptionalities, and helps professionals obtain the conditions and resources necessary for effective professional practice.

Department of Vocational Rehabilitation (DVR)

(Check the Internet to find a DVR in your area.)

The mission of the DVR is to provide services and advocacy to assist people with disabilities to live independently, obtain employment, and enjoy equality in the communities in which they live and work. The DVR works in partnership with consumers and other stakeholders to provide services and advocacy resulting in employment, independent living, and equality for individuals with disabilities.

Division on Career Development and Transition (DCDT)

http://www.dcdt.org

A subdivision of CEC, DCDT focuses on career development and transition for youth with disabilities, promotes national and international efforts to improve the quality of and access to career/vocational and transition services, increases the participation of education in career development and transition goals, and influences policies affecting career development and transition services for people with disabilities. DCDT publishes the journal *Career Development for Exceptional Individuals*, sponsors state subdivisions, and offers state and national conferences on career development and transition for youth with disabilities.

Division for Culturally and Linguistically Diverse Exceptional Learners (DDEL) of CEC

http://www.ddelcec.org/

DDEL is one of the special interest groups of the *Council for Exceptional Children* (CEC). DDEL is the only professional organization dedicated exclusively to the concerns of culturally and linguistically diverse exceptional learners.

Social Security Administration (SSA)

http://www.socialsecurity.gov

The SSA operates the federally funded program that provides benefits for people of any age who are unable to work because of a severe mental or physical disability. There are several programs for people with disabilities, including Social Security Disability Insurance, Supplemental Security Income, Plan to Achieve Self-Support, Medicaid, and Medicare. For local information, contact your local SSA.

Web Sites

Directory of Independent Living Centers Nationwide

http://www.virtualcil.net/cils

This site provides a map of the United States with links to centers for independent living that provide services in the areas of advocacy, independent living skills training, information and referral, and peer counseling.

The Equity Alliance at ASU (Arizona State University)

http://www.equityallianceatasu.org/

Building on educational theory, cutting-edge research, and the momentum of the National Center for Culturally Responsive Educational Systems, the National Center for Urban School Improvement, and NIUSI-LeadScape, the ambition of the Equity Alliance at ASU is to promote equity, access, and participation in education.

Family Village

http://www.familyvillage.wisc.edu

The Family Village web site brings together thousands of online resources in an organized, easy-to-use directory. The centerpiece of Family Village is the library, where children and adults with disabilities, their families, and their friends and allies can find information on more than 300 diagnoses.

Family Voices

http://www.familyvoices.org

Family Voices aims to achieve family-centered care for all children and youth with special health care needs and/or disabilities. Through their national network, they provide families with the tools to make informed decisions, advocate for improved public and private policies, build partnerships among professionals and families, and serve as a trusted resource on health care.

IDEA Partnership

http://www.ideapartnership.org

The IDEA Partnership reflects the collaborative work of more than 50 national organizations, technical assistance providers, and organizations and agencies at state and local levels. Together with the Office of Special Education Programs, the Partner Organizations form a community with the potential to transform the way we work and improve outcomes for students and youth with disabilities.

National Association for Parents of Children with Visual Impairments (NAPVI)

http://www.spedex.com/napvi/

NAPVI is a nonprofit organization of, by, and for parents committed to providing support to the parents of children who have visual impairments. This national organization enables parents to find information and resources for their children who are blind or visually impaired, including those with additional disabilities. NAPVI provides leadership, support, and training to assist parents in helping their children reach their potential.

National Coalition for Parent Involvement in Education (NCPIE)

http://www.ncpie.org

The mission of NCPIE is to advocate for the involvement of parents and families in their children's education and to foster relationships among home, school, and community to enhance the education of all young people.

National Council on Independent Living (NCIL)

http://www.ncil.org

As a membership organization, NCIL advances independent living and the rights of people with disabilities through consumer-driven advocacy. NCIL envisions a world in which people with disabilities are valued equally and participate fully.

National Dissemination Center for Children with Disabilities (NICHCY)

http://www.nichcy.org

Offering a wealth of information on disabilities, NICHCY serves the nation as a central source of information on disabilities in infants, toddlers, children, and youth including easy-to-read information on IDEA, State Resource Sheets to help connect with the disability agencies and organizations in each state, as well as many articles and publications.

National Down Syndrome Congress (NDSC)

http://www.ndsccenter.org

The mission of the NDSC is to provide information, advocacy, and support concerning all aspects of life for individuals with Down syndrome. The vision of the NDSC is a world with equal rights and opportunities for people with Down syndrome. It is the purpose of the NDSC to create a national climate in which all people recognize and embrace the value and dignity of people with Down syndrome.

National Federation of Families for Children's Mental Health

http://www.ffcmh.org

This national family-run organization provides advocacy at the national level for the rights of children and youth with emotional, behavioral, and mental health challenges and their families; provides leadership and technical assistance to a nationwide network of family-run organizations; and collaborates with family-run and other child-serving organizations to transform mental health care in America.

National Secondary Transition Technical Assistance Center

http://www.nsttac.org

> This center provides support and information to states, local education agencies, practitioners, educators, parents, and students regarding effective transition education that can enhance postschool outcomes for youth with disabilities.

National Youth Leadership Network (NYLN)

http://nyln.org

> NYLN provides a national voice for young leaders with disabilities and offers resources and speakers on a variety of disability-related topics.

PACER Center

http://www.PACER.org

> The mission of PACER (Parent Advocacy Coalition for Educational Rights) Center is to expand opportunities and enhance the quality of life of children and young adults with disabilities and their families, and is based on the concept of parents helping parents.

Technical Assistance ALLIANCE for Parent Centers

http://www.taalliance.org

> The ALLIANCE is an innovative partnership of one national and six regional parent technical assistance centers, each funded by the U.S. Department of Education's Office of Special Education Programs. These seven projects compose a unified technical assistance system for the purpose of developing, assisting, and coordinating the more than 100 Parent Training and Information Centers and Community Parent Resource Centers established under IDEA. The national and regional parent technical assistance centers work to strengthen the connections to the larger OSEP Technical Assistance and Dissemination Network and fortify partnerships between Parent Centers and education systems at local, state, and national levels.

Technical Assistance on Transition and the Rehabilitation Act (TATRA)

http://www.pacer.org/tatra/

> PACER's TATRA Project provides information and training on transition planning, the adult service system, and strategies that prepare youth for successful employment, postsecondary education, and independent living outcomes.

Training and Advocacy Support Center (TASC) at National Disability Rights Network

http://www.napas.org/en/about/faqs.html

> TASC is a centralized repository for training and technical assistance information and coordination for federally mandated Protection and Advocacy (P&A) Programs and operates on the principles of equality, equity, fairness, independence, cultural competency and more.

Transition Coalition

http://www.transitioncoalition.org/transition/module_home.php

> Located at the University of Kansas, Department of Special Education, the Transition Coalition maximizes professional development focusing on secondary school reform and transition at the national, state, and local levels. Secondary Transition and Cultural Diversity is

a FREE research-based online training module that provides comprehensive information on how culture intrinsically influences people and systems, the many ways that culture intercepts with transition services, and the differences in values and perceptions of disability that can affect how families consider services.

Transition Resources for CLD Families of Youth with Disabilities

http://www.virtualcil.net/cils

This web site provides a directory of independent living centers nationwide.

Index

Page numbers followed by *t* indicate tables; those followed by *f* indicate figures.

Accountability, 103
Acculturation, 19, 20
Action research, 98, 105–107, 113, 116
    see also Data-based decision making
Advocates
    parent support groups, 46–47
    for parent training, 41
    parents as, 25*t*, 26
    students for themselves, 45
African Americans
    alienation of in education process, 9
    communication culture of, 33
    labeling issues of, 18–19
    liability of culture, 8–9, 15
    NLTS study on, 2, 2*t*–3*t*
    possible reasons for noninvolvement, 9, 15, 38–39
    poverty rates of, 4
    stereotyping of, 8–9, 16
ALLIANCE, *see* Technical Assistance ALLIANCE for
    Parent Centers
American Indians
    communication culture of, 33
    liability of culture, 8–9
    poverty rates of, 4
    views on children with disabilities, 7, 11, 18
American society, *see* Society, United States
Americans with Disabilities Act of 1990 (PL 101-336), 58,
    66, 71, 85
Arizona State University, 110
Asian American/Canadians
    communication culture of, 33
    deference to authority issues and, 18, 26, 33
    feelings of lack of respect, 9–10
    immigration issues of, 17
    law and policy understanding, 14
    poverty rates of, 4
    preference to informal approaches, 42
    views on children with disabilities, 9–10, 11
Assessment
    in cultural competence, 39, 50–54
    parental, 25*t*, 26
    see also Transition assessment

Authority
    cultural deference to, 18, 20, 26, 33
    during skilled dialogue, 28
    taken by professionals, 38
    see also Power, balance of

Background information, learning, 7*t*, 34, 42*t*, 48, 59
Barriers in transition planning
    case sample (Lucias Washington), 11–13
    case sample (Lupe Espinosa), 5–6, 8–9, 10–11
    generational conflicts, 19–20
    immigration issues, 16–17
    lack of cultural understanding, 6–9, 15–16, 18–19, 119
    lack of legal understanding, 14–15, 119
    lack of respect, 9–11, 119
    language issues, 17–18, 39, 119
    research findings on, 118–119
    stereotyping, 15–16, 119
    training about, 38–39
    unacknowledged hopes and dreams, 10–13
    use of cultural reciprocity to breakdown, 29
    see also CLD families with youth with disabilities; Non-
        involvement; School personnel; Schools; Transition
        planning
Basic survival needs, 4, 7*t*, 15, 16, 20
Beliefs, *see* Values
Bias, awareness of
    lack of, 10
    professional development in, 38–39
    for successful collaboration, 7*t*, 109–110
    using cultural reciprocity, 28–29

California Department of Education, 69
CEC, *see* Council for Exceptional Children
CEUs, *see* Continuing education units
Chinese American/Canadians, *see* Asian American/Canadians
Chinese Parents Association for the Disabled (CPAD), 46
The Choicemaker Self-Determination Transition Curriculum
    (Martin and Marshall, 1994), 43*t*
"Circle of friends," 35, 35*f*, 62
CLD (cultural and linguistic diversity)
    examples of disrespect and disregard for, 6, 7–8

supportive literature for, 6t
uses of term, 3–4
CLD families with youth with disabilities
  case sample on input from (Cho Hee Dan), 71–72
  case sample on multiple roles of (Wen Lee), 25–26
  choosing transition program, 67–71
  collaboration with, 109–110, 121
  effective communication with, 32–33
  getting perspectives of, 84
  importance of cultural understanding of, 7t, 20
  as only "consent-givers," 24–25
  roles of, 25–26, 25t
  studies on construct of, 2
  support groups for, 46–47
  supportive literature for working with, 32t
  training for, 39–42
  see also Barriers in transition planning; Family; Parent
    training
CLD youth with disabilities
  achieving quality adult life, 1–2
  case sample on input from (Cho Hee Dan), 71–72
  expectations of, 8, 15–16, 18–19
  IDEA requirements to consider preferences of, 57–58
  input from, 23, 35, 49, 83f, 86, 91
  liability of culture, 8–9
  self-determination training and, 43–45, 45t
Collaboration
  with CLD families, 109–110, 121
  creating with no cultural affiliation, 29
  cultural responsiveness in, 27–31
  in the family-centered approach, 34
  key elements of, 24–27, 24t
  for professional development, 102
  in professional learning communities, 103–104
  through person-centered planning, 62
  for transition assessment, 59
Commitment, 24t
Communication
  with CLD families, 32–33
  different styles in, 33, 51
  in the family-centered approach, 34
  as key element to collaboration, 24–31, 24t
  in person-centered planning, 33–36
  professional development in, 39, 103
  supportive literature in, 32t
Community
  cultural differences in value of, 7, 30
  as part of a quality adult life, 1
  as part of the family's strength, 47
  transition agencies in, 69, 71
  see also Professional learning communities (PLCs)
Community liaison
  to assist in parent training, 37, 41–42, 46–47, 120
  Fiesta Educativa, 121
  supportive literature on, 32t
Community Parent Resource Centers (CPRCs), 47
Continuing education units (CEUs), 107
Council for Exceptional Children (CEC), 43, 59, 66
CPAD, see Chinese Parents Association for the Disabled)
The Crosswalks Intervention, 111
Cultural affiliation, lack of, 29, 30–31
Cultural and linguistic diversity, see CLD

Cultural bumps, 4, 6–9, 18, 20
Cultural competence
  aspects of, 26–27
  as key element to collaboration, 24t, 26–31
  necessity of, 119
  professional development in, 37–39, 40f, 50–54
  supportive literature for, 32t
Cultural diversity, 3–4
Cultural insensitivity, 15–16, 38
Cultural mismatch theory, 19–20
Cultural reciprocity
  barriers to using, 29
  case sample in (George Polomalu), 30–31
  case sample in (large Hispanic population school), 36–37
  features of, 28
  process for use of, 29–30
  supportive literature for, 32t, 39
  in transition planning, 32–33
Cultural responsiveness
  example of, 61–62
  necessity of, 119
  professional learning communities and, 104–105
  questions to assist with, 27, 48–49
  recommended practices in, 31–32, 32t
  skilled dialogue and, 28
  supportive literature for, 32t
  in the transition IEP and SOP, 73, 74f
Cultural views
  differences in, 18–19, 119
  on education, 9–10, 16, 40
  as a liability, 6–9, 6t
  self-determination programs and, 45
  on types of contact preferred, 41–42
Culturally responsive transition planning, see Transition
    planning

Data-based decision making, 98
  see also Action research
Disability Support Services (DSS), 71
Discrimination, 15–16
Disrespect of cultural diversity, 6, 8–10
Division on Career Development and Transition (DCDT),
    43, 59, 66
Dreams, see Hopes and dreams
Drop-out rates, 56

Education, see General education
Education for All Handicapped Children Act of 1975
    (PL 94-142), 56, 112
Employment, 1–2, 2t–3t, 4
Empowerment
  case sample (Alvarado High School), 98–100, 106, 114–115
  need for, 115
  of youth through self-determination, 43
  see also Teacher empowerment
English proficiency, see Language issues
Environment for transition assessment, 59, 75f
Expectations of CLD youth, 8, 15–16, 18–19
  see also Stereotyping

Family, 1, 19
  see also CLD families with youth with disabilities

Family-centered approach, 32t, 33–36, 48
Fiesta Educativa, 120–122
Free appropriate public education (FAPE), 56, 57

General education
    as part of a quality adult life, 1
    poverty and, 4
    self-determination training and, 43t
    student access to, 11
Generational conflicts, 6t, 19–20
George Washington University, 107, 109t
Graduation rates, 56–57

Health care, 1, 4
Higher Education Consortium for Special Education, 66
Hispanics
    communication culture of, 33
    cultural values of, 7, 10, 19, 122
    feelings of lack of respect, 9
    immigration issues of, 17
    law and policy understanding, 14
    liability of culture, 8–9
    NLTS study on, 2, 2t–3t
    possible reasons for noninvolvement, 18, 36
    poverty rates of, 4
    preference to informal approaches, 41–42
    stereotyping of, 8–9, 16
    views on children with disabilities, 7–8, 120
Home-based activities, 10, 37
    see also Meetings
Hopes and dreams
    considering in transition assessment, 61–62
    encouraging sharing of, 7t
    supportive literature on, 6t
    typical American, 1
    unacknowledged, 6, 10–13, 118
    see also Postsecondary goals
Housing, 1, 4
Human decency, 23, 24

IDEALS framework (O'Hair, McLaughlin, and Reitzug, 2000), 105
IEP, see Individualized education program (IEP)
Immigration issues, 6t, 16–17, 20
    see also Undocumented families
Independent living, 2t, 10, 19
Individualism, 45
Individualized education program (IEP), 27, 44, 64, 65t
Individuals with Disabilities Act Amendments of 1997 (PL 105-17), 57, 68
Individuals with Disabilities Education Act (IDEA) of 1990 (PL 101-476), 11, 57, 68
Individuals with Disabilities Education Act (IDEA) of 2004 (PL 108-446)
    age for transition planning, 55
    SOP format under, 66
    transition IEP under, 67
    transition requirements of, 57–58, 68, 84
Insensitivity, 15–16, 38
Intergenerational conflicts, see Generational conflicts
Interpreters, 33, 41, 109, 120
Iowa Department of Education, 63
Iowa Model for Transition Assessments, 63–64, 65t, 77, 79f
I-Plan (Van-Reusen and Boss, 1990), 43t
Jargon, 38

Labeling, 3, 6t, 18–19
Language issues
    lack of proficiency, 6t, 17–18, 20, 37
    in meetings, 27, 119
Latinos, see Hispanics
Laws and policies
    assumptions of shared values in, 7
    lack of understanding of, 12–15, 39, 119
    mandating professional development, 101
    providing information on, 7t, 14–15
    student knowledge of, 44
    supportive literature on, 6t
Leadership
    characteristics associated with, 95, 95t
    promoting in parents, 122
    through teacher empowerment, 97–100
    transformational, 96
    see also Teacher leadership
Learning communities, 97–98, 103–105
Learning Disabilities Association of America, 66
Literacy, limited, 17–18

Mainstreaming, 112
Making the Match (Sitlington, Neubert, Begun, Lombard, and Leconte, 1996), 62–63, 64f, 73, 75f
MAPS (Making Action Plans; Falvey, Forest, Pearpoint, & Rosenburg, 1997), 35–36, 49, 62
Martinez, Irene, 120–122
Meetings
    authority issues during, 18, 20, 26, 33
    communication issues during, 33
    encouraging participation of parents during, 39–40, 109
    encouraging participation of students during, 44
    interpreters for, 27, 33, 41, 109, 120
    language issues during, 17–18
    providing basic information about, 15
    sensitivity to timing of, 7t, 15, 20, 38, 109
    settings for, 37, 41–42
    see also Home-based activities
Mentors, 46–47, 120
Minorities, 1–2, 2t–3t

National Center on Secondary Education and Transition, 107
National Longitudinal Transition Studies (NLTS-1 and NLTS-2), 1–2, 2t–3t, 56–57
National Transition Documentation Summit, 66
Native Americans, see American Indians
Next S.T.E.P. (Halpern, et al, 1997), 43t
Noninvolvement, 9–10, 15, 18, 36, 39–40, 119
    see also Barriers in transition planning

Office of Special Education Programs (OSEP), 47, 110

Pacific Islanders, 4, 33
Parent support groups, 25t, 26, 46–47, 120
Parent training
    availability of, 120
    community liaisons and, 37, 41–42, 46–47, 120
    in leadership, 122
    to promote active participation, 39–42
    sample agenda in, 41f
    on transitioning, 39–42
    see also CLD families with disabled youth

Parent Training and Information Centers (PTIs), 47

Parents, *see* CLD families with youth with disabilities

Pathways to Successful Transition Model (Kochhar-Bryant and Greene, 2003, 2009), 68–69, 69*t*, 77, 84

Person-centered planning (PCP)
  case sample, 36–37
  collaboration in, 62
  communication in, 33–36
  studies in, 34–35
  supportive literature for, 32*t*

Personnel, *see* School personnel

PL 101-336 (Americans with Disabilities Act of 1990), 58, 66, 71, 85

PL 101-476 (Individuals with Disabilities Education Act of 1990), 11, 57, 68

PL 105-17 (Individuals with Disabilities Act Amendments of 1997), 57, 68

PL 105-220 (Rehabilitation Act Amendments of 1998), 71

PL 108-446, *see* Individuals with Disabilities Education Act (IDEA) of 2004 (PL 108-446)

PL 93-112 (Rehabilitation Act of 1973), 58, 66, 85

PL 94-142 (Education for All Handicapped Children Act of 1975), 56, 112

Postsecondary goals
  case sample (Juan Carlos Martinez), 76*f*
  cultural differences in, 7*t*, 24
  generational conflicts in, 19–20
  including in the SOP form, 81*f*, 82*f*, 86
  reciprocity in, 28
  in the transition IEP, 77, 78*f*
  see also Hopes and dreams; Transition planning

Postsecondary school attendance
  NLTS information on, 2, 2*t*–3*t*
  poverty rates and, 4
  resources for, 71
  students with disabilities and, 56–57
  teacher opportunities for, 107

Poverty rates, 4, 57

Power, balance of, 24–26, 24*t*, 28, 38
  see also Authority

Powers, Kristen, 108–111

Principals, role of, 111, 115

Professional development
  in communication, 39
  continuing higher education for, 107–111
  in cultural competence, 37–39, 40*f*, 50–54
  Dr. Bill Beacham interview on, 101–103
  Dr. Kristen Powers interview on role of, 108–111
  to enable organizational change, 113
  essential components of, 101
  to promote teacher leadership, 100–101, 108*t*, 116
  see also Training

Professional learning communities (PLCs), 103–105, 116
  see also Community

PTIs, *see* Parent Training and Information Centers

Quality adult life, 1–2, 2*t*–3*t*, 4

Questions
  culturally responsive, 27, 48–49
  to guide transition assessment, 59, 61–62, 63*f*
  to learn family background, 34
  MAPS, 36

Reciprocity, *see* Cultural reciprocity

Recreation, 1

Rehabilitation Act Amendments of 1998 (PL 105-220), 71

Rehabilitation Act of 1973 (PL 93-112), 58, 66, 85

Relationships
  building during professional development, 102–103
  enabling organization change, 113
  establishing informally, 42*t*
  forming positive, 24
  questions to help develop, 48–49, 59

Report presentation, parental, 25*t*, 26

Resources
  to assist in promoting teacher empowerment, 98
  needed for leadership training, 110
  for professional development, 100
  to promote organizational change, 113

Respect
  as key element to collaboration, 24*t*
  lack of from school personnel, 9–10, 15–16, 118
  skilled dialogue and, 27–28
  supportive literature on, 6*t*

Roles
  of the parents, 25–26, 25*t*
  of the principal, 97–98, 100

Salaries, 1, 107, 116

School personnel
  biases of, 15–16
  skill levels needed, 68, 69
  understanding barriers, 9
  see also Barriers in transition planning

Schools
  developing parental knowledge, 53–54
  gaining staff input, 113
  promoting leadership in, 111
  promoting organizational change in, 112–115, 113*t*
  see also Barriers in transition planning; Meetings

Section 504 of the Rehabilitation Act Amendments (PL 105-220), 71

Section 504 of the Rehabilitation Act of 1973 (PL 93-112), 58, 66, 85

Self-advocacy, 45

Self-determination
  differing cultural conceptions in, 19
  generational conflicts from, 20
  person-centered planning (PCP) and, 35
  for a quality adult life, 1–2
  student developing, 45*t*
  supportive literature for, 32*t*, 43*t*
  training in, 43–45

Self-Determination Synthesis Project, 45

Self-reflection, 29, 98

Skilled dialogue, 27–28, 32–33

Skilled Dialogue: Strategies for Responding to Cultural Diversity in Early Childhood (Barrera and Corso, 2003), 39

Society, United States, 1, 6–9

Socioeconomic status (SES)
  as a barrier, 20
  sensitivity to, 15, 38
  teacher leadership and, 95
  transition outcomes and, 4

SOP, *see* Summary of Functional Performance

Special education programs, 56

Staff development, *see* Professional development

Steps to Self-Determination (Field and Hoffman, 1996), 43*t*

Stereotyping
   avoiding with cultural reciprocity, 28
   as a barrier, 8–9, 15–16, 38, 119
   limiting respect of cultural diversity, 3
   by school professionals, 8–9, 15–16
   supportive literature on, 6*t*
   see also expectations of CLD youth
Students, *see* CLD youth with disabilities
Summary of Functional Performance (SOP)
   case sample (Qui Tran), 65–66, 79, 80*f*–83*f,* 84
   culturally responsive, 73, 74*f*
   history of, 66
   instructions for use of, 66–67, 85–86
   legal requirements in, 57–58
   purpose of, 55–56, 58, 66, 84
   template of, 87–91
Support groups, 32*t,* 41, 41*f,* 46–47, 120–122

TAKE CHARGE for the Future (Powers, Ellison,
      Matuszewski, Wilson and Turner, 1997), 43*t*
Teacher empowerment, 97–100
   see also Empowerment
Teacher leadership
   case sample (Alvarado High School), 98–100
   characteristics of, 94–96, 95*t*
   professional learning communities (PLCs) and, 103–105
   promoting change and, 112–115
   promoting in public schools, 96
   through action research, 105–107
   through continuing higher education, 107–111
   through professional development, 100–101
   through teacher empowerment, 97–100
   using influence of, 114
   see also Leadership
Teachers
   advance training in transition planning, 107–111
   issues faced by, 93–94, 115
   role in self-determination training for students, 43–44
   salary compensation for higher education, 107, 116
Technical Assistance ALLIANCE for Parent Centers
      (ALLIANCE), 47
Training, *see* Parent training; Professional development
Transformational leadership, 96
Transition assessment
   case sample (James Montgomery), 78*f*
   case sample (Juan Carlos Martinez), 60–61, 73, 75*f,* 76*f,* 77*f*
   collaboration in, 59
   compared to traditional assessment, 59–60
   considering hopes and dreams in, 61–62
   defined, 58–59
   developing a plan for, 61–62
   importance of, 66
   knowledge and skill domains for, 62*f*
   person-centered, 62
   planning form for, 63*f,* 64*f*
   purpose of, 84
   see also Assessment
Transition individualized education program (transition IEP)
   case sample (George Polomalu), 30–31
   case sample (James Montgomery), 76–77, 78*f,* 79
   case sample (Juan Carlos Martinez), 76*f*
   case sample (Lucias Washington), 11–13
   crucial roles in development of, 23
   cultural responsiveness in, 73, 74*f*

   defined under IDEA, 57
   format of, 67, 84
   legal requirements for, 57–58
   purpose of, 55–56, 58, 84
   questions to help develop, 27
   template of, 92
Transition outcomes, 2, 4
Transition planning
   case sample (Cho Hee Dan), 71–72
   case sample (Lupe Espinosa), 5–6, 8–9, 10–11
   CLD family experiences in, 4–6
   cultural reciprocity and communication in, 32–33
   family-centered approach in, 33–36
   higher education in, 107–111
   home-based activities in, 10
   implementing information in, 122–123
   legal requirements in, 57–58
   professional development and, 50–54
   professional learning communities (PLCs) and, 104–105
   promoting parent participation in, 39, 109
   questions to help develop, 48–49
   recommended practices in, 7*t,* 31–32
   student input in, 23, 35, 49, 83*f,* 86
   suggestions for professionals in, 119–120
   teacher education in, 107, 108*t*
   traditional, 33
   types of programs for, 67–71
   see also Barriers in transition planning; Postsecondary
      goals; Transition IEP
Transition services
   agencies that assist with, 69, 70*f,* 71
   case sample (Juan Carlos Martinez), 76*f*
   culturally sensitive, 28, 39
   IDEA and, 57
   immigration issues and, 17
   influences to determining, 68
   in the transition IEP, 78*f*
Transition to Adult Living: An Information and Reference Guide
      (California Dept. of Education, 2007), 69, 70*f*
Trust
   in the family-centered approach, 34
   immigration issues and, 17
   importance of building, 7*t*
   as key element to collaboration, 24*t*
   of teacher leaders, 113

Undocumented families, 17
   see also Immigration issues
University of Kansas, 107, 109*t*
U.S. Department of Education, 47, 67, 111

Values
   comparing using cultural reciprocity, 29
   cultural differences in, 6, 7*t,* 11, 38, 45
   family, 19
   generational conflicts in, 19–20
   in the transformational teacher, 96
Vocational rehabilitation, 56
Vocational Rehabilitation Comprehensive Assessment, 85

Whites
   NLTS study on, 2, 2*t*–3*t*
   outcomes for, 57
   poverty rates, 4